ENTERING ADULTHOOD:

Looking at Body Image and Eating Disorders

ENTERING ADULTHOOD:

Looking at Body Image and Eating Disorders

A Curriculum for Grades 9-12

Susan Giarratano, EdD, MSPH, CHES

Contemporary Health Series
Kathleen Middleton, MS, Series Editor

Network Publications, a division of ETR Associates
Santa Cruz, CA • 1991

Network Publications' Contemporary Health Series

Into Adolescence (for grades 5-8)

Choosing Abstinence
Enhancing Self-Esteem
Learning About AIDS
Learning About Reproduction and Birth
Living in a Family
A Time of Change (puberty)
Avoiding Drugs
Communicating Emotions
Becoming a Health-Wise Consumer
Making and Keeping Friends
Living Without Tobacco
Actions for Wellpower
Caring for Our Planet and Our Health
A Menu for Good Health

Entering Adulthood (for grades 9-12)

Connecting Health, Communication and Self-Esteem
Coping with Sexual Pressures
Living in Relationships
Preventing Sexually Related Disease
Understanding Reproduction, Birth and Contraception
Balancing Stress for Success
Understanding Depression and Suicide
Examining Drugs and Risks
Developing Responsibility and Self-Discipline
Planning Life Directions
Creating a Healthy Environment
Moving into Fitness
Looking at Body Image and Eating Disorders

 Published by Network Publications,
P.O. Box 1830, Santa Cruz, CA 95061-1830.

Printed in the United States of America

10 9 8 7 6 5 4 3 2 1

Cover design: Julia Chiapella

Illustrations: Ann Smiley

Title No. 397

Library of Congress Cataloging-in-Publication Data

Giarratano, Susan.
Entering adulthood : looking at body image and eating disorders : a curriculum for grades 9-12 / Susan Giarratano.
p. cm. — (Contemporary health series)
Includes bibliographical references (p.).
ISBN 1-56071-050-0
1. Eating disorders—Study and teaching. 2. Body image—Study and teaching 3. Self-respect—Study and teaching. I. Title. II. Series.
RC552.E18G53 1991 90-22190
616.85'26'00712—dc20 CIP

This curriculum was made possible, in part, by a grant from the Walter S. Johnson Foundation. The opinions expressed in this curriculum are those of the author and do not necessarily reflect the opinions of the Walter S. Johnson Foundation.

CONTENTS

EDITOR'S PREFACE
Contemporary Health Series

Health educators and practitioners know that prevention of health problems is far more desirable than treatment. The earlier the knowledge and skill to make healthful decisions are instilled, the greater the chance a healthful lifestyle will be adopted. School is the logical place in our society to provide children, adolescents and young adults the learning opportunities essential to developing the knowledge and skills to choose a healthful life course.

The **Contemporary Health Series** has been designed to provide educators with the curricular tools necessary to challenge students to take personal responsibility for their health. The long-range goals for the **Contemporary Health Series** are as follows:

Cognitive. Students will recognize the function of the existing body of knowledge pertaining to health and family life education.
Affective. Students will experience personal growth in the development of a positive self-concept and the ability to interact with others.
Practice. Students will gain skill in acting on personal decisions about health-related life choices.

Within the **Contemporary Health Series** there are two curricular divisions: Into Adolescence for middle school teachers and Entering Adulthood for high school teachers. The Into Adolescence modules focus on several different health and family life topics. Modules addressing puberty, AIDS, the family, self-esteem, reproduction and birth, sexual abstinence, and drug, alcohol and tobacco education have been developed by skilled author/educators.

Entering Adulthood includes reproduction, birth and contraception, health behavior, communication and self-esteem, AIDS and other STDs, relationships, sexual abstinence, and drug, alcohol and tobacco education.

All the authors are, or have been, classroom teachers with particular expertise in each of the topic areas. They bring a unique combination of theory, content and practice resulting in curricula which weave educational learning theory into lessons appropriate for the developmental age of the student. The module format was chosen to facilitate flexibility as the modules are compatible with each other but may stand alone. Finally, ease of use by the classroom teacher has driven the design. The lessons are comprehensive, key components are clearly identified and masters for all student and teacher materials are provided.

The **Contemporary Health Series** is intended to help teachers address critical health issues in their classrooms. The beneficiaries are their students, our children, and the next generation.

Kathleen Middleton, MS, CHES
Series Editor

INTRODUCTION

Americans are obsessed with appearance. Slenderness is a major preoccupation in our society. This preoccupation has produced a population overly concerned with body fat and overweight. It has also produced a multimillion-dollar diet industry.

Preoccupation with body image is evident in the tabloids at the checkout counters of supermarkets. Weight reduction clinics, programs and products have multiplied. They promise glamour, financial and personal benefits, as well as weight loss.

The media contributes to this fascination with thinness with advertisements and programs that feature slender, well-proportioned females and lean males with well-defined muscles. Even television newscasters look like models. High-fashion models are often role-models for girls. Most female high fashion models are so slender that it is difficult to determine their ages. The use of preadolescent and adolescent females as models further emphasizes the young and slender ideal.

Sports figures are often role models for boys. Most sports figures are extremely muscular and well-proportioned. For men, the athletic-looking body is idealized.

Overweight people are usually depicted in the media for humorous purposes or weight control promotions. They are also depicted as gluttons, which research indicates is a myth. The people who are shown as living desirable, rewarding lives are slender and good-looking. These messages affect perceptions of body image for everyone—adults, children and adolescents.

Children as young as five years old are preoccupied with dieting because they fear being fat. A recent study examined attitudes among third through sixth graders from middle-income neighborhoods. It found that a large percentage of eight- to thirteen-year-old boys and girls wanted to be thinner and said they had already tried to lose weight.

Most adolescents are preoccupied with the physical and biological changes in their bodies. This is quite normal. During adolescence they are also developing mental and emotional coping mechanisms to deal with those changes. Some dieting behaviors among adolescents may be considered within the range of normal. But obsession with the pursuit of thinness and the control of weight may be a severe psychological problem that needs competent professional assistance.

The federal government has recently published *Healthy People 2000: National Health Promotion and Disease Objectives.* Some of these objectives address the concern for individuals who are underweight and may have associated health problems. Total food composition and consumption and exercise behaviors are addressed in the objectives. Eating and exercise behaviors associated with psychological problems, such as anorexia nervosa, bulimia and compulsive overeating, are specified in related mental health objectives.

Overview

This module focuses on issues related to body image and self-esteem, eating disorders and sensible eating habits for adolescents. The content and learning activities will enable students to identify positive attitudes and perceptions about self- and body image, both from an individual and peer perspective. A more accurate assessment of personal body image should result.

The module includes an overview of eating disorders with indicators of each disorder and resources for help. This is followed by a review of sensible and practical eating habits from childhood through adulthood, with particular emphasis on the importance of nutrition during adolescence.

Objectives

Lesson 1 *Body Image and Self-Esteem*

- Students will be able to define body image.
- Students will be able to identify influences on attitudes about body image.
- Students will be able to evaluate body image to clarify positive personal traits.

Lesson 2	*Pressures on Body Image*	■ Students will be able to evaluate body image messages in advertising. ■ Students will be able to list realistic ways to improve body image.
Lesson 3	*Eating Disorders*	■ Students will be able to identify the characteristics of anorexia nervosa and bulimia. ■ Students will be able to explain the relationship between eating disorders and body image.
Lesson 4	*Help for Eating Disorders*	■ Students will be able to illustrate prevention behaviors for eating disorders. ■ Students will be able to differentiate between normal teen-age eating behaviors and eating disorder behaviors.
Lesson 5	*Weight Control Problems*	■ Students will be able to differentiate between effective and ineffective weight control programs. ■ Students will be able to identify community resources for weight control.
Lesson 6	*Sensible Eating Habits*	■ Students will be able to identify sensible eating and exercise behaviors. ■ Students will be able to identify society's influences on eating behaviors.

Time

The time indicated for each lesson is an approximate measure, based on a 45-50 minute class period. The actual time required to complete all activities in a given lesson will vary, depending on student interest and ability. Lessons that will probably require more than one class period to complete are indicated.

Instructional Strategies

This module incorporates a variety of instructional strategies designed to develop and maintain student interest and motivation. Some strategies are traditional, while others are more interactive, encouraging students to help each other learn. The specific strategies used in each lesson are clearly identified. An alphabetical list of instructional strategies and their descriptions follows:

Case Studies	Overhead Transparencies
Class Discussion	Teacher Lecture
Cooperative Learning Groups	Worksheets

Case Studies

Case studies are written histories of a problem or situation that students read, discuss and analyze. This is a good way to encourage student involvement and to center discussion on practical issues.

Class Discussion

A class discussion led by the teacher is one of the most valuable strategies used in education. It can be used to initiate, amplify or summarize a lesson. Most of the lessons in this module include some form of class discussion.

Cooperative Learning Groups

Cooperative learning is one of the most common and effective strategies used in this module. Students work in small groups to disseminate and share information, analyze ideas or solve problems. The size of the group depends on the nature of the lesson and the make-up of the class. Groups work best with from two to six members.

Group structure will affect the success of the lessons. Groups can be formed by student choice, random selection or a more formal, teacher-influenced process. Groups seem to function best when they represent the variety and balance found in the classroom. Groups also work better when each student has a responsibility within the group (reader, recorder, timer, reporter, etc.).

While groups are working on their tasks, the teacher should move from group to group, answering questions and dealing with any problems that arise. At the conclusion of the group process, some closure should take place.

Overhead Transparencies

Overhead transparencies are an effective visual aid to use in presenting information and graphic examples. Most of the lessons in this module provide teacher resources that can be used as transparencies.

Teacher Lecture

A traditional teacher lecture disseminates information directly from the teacher to students. In some lessons, this approach is the best way to provide information. Generally, this method is combined with other methods to assure high-level motivation and learning.

Worksheets

Most lessons in this module include worksheets. Students may be asked to complete the worksheets individually or in cooperative learning groups. Some worksheets include an activity to be completed outside of class. Completed worksheets should generally be reviewed with the whole class to provide relevant and timely feedback.

Teacher Responsibilities

The subject of this module, body image and eating disorders, is a sensitive one, and the teaching of it must be approached carefully. Be aware of the maturity level of your students and adjust lesson activities and content accordingly. Involve students' family members as appropriate.

Classroom atmosphere is critical when teaching sensitive topics. You are encouraged to establish classroom conditions and groundrules that contribute to feelings of security, autonomy, belonging, purpose and personal competence.

If possible, for discussions involving the whole class, seating should be arranged in a circle or horseshoe configuration, so all students can see their classmates. Such arrangements encourage interaction and promote a more relaxed environment.

Groundrules help provide a comfortable, positive and secure classroom environment. You may choose to involve students in developing class groundrules. Some suggestions for groundrules include:

- Treat each other with respect and courtesy.
- Listen carefully to others.
- Allow others to speak without interruption.
- Be supportive of others.
- No put-downs allowed.

Students should be assured from the beginning that they have the right to pass during any discussion or activity that involves personal opinions, feelings or experiences. *Be sensitive to student feelings, and provide privacy for personal assessments.* Be prepared to refer students to professional help or counseling for problem eating behaviors or concerns about body image.

Evaluative Methods

Each lesson provides the teacher with one or more methods for evaluating student performance on stated objectives. The methods are listed following the procedure section of each lesson. Evaluative methods include analysis and comment on worksheets and other written materials, as well as observation of individual responses.

It is impossible to objectively, quantitatively or qualitatively measure the development and maintenance of personal eating behaviors, and it is inappropriate to grade student work that is reflective of individual feelings, beliefs or behaviors. Therefore, the evaluation methods serve as tools to assess students' participation and cognitive learning from each lesson.

LESSON 1

BODY IMAGE AND SELF-ESTEEM

Objectives

Students will be able to define body image.

Students will be able to identify influences on attitudes about body image.

Students will be able to evaluate body image to clarify positive personal traits.

Time

One class period.

Overview

Students need to be aware of and understand the importance of self-esteem and a positive body image in achieving personal health. In this lesson, students examine influences on body image. They then assess their personal traits and trade assessments with peers.

Teacher Materials and Preparation

COPY:

✓ **What's Perfect?** worksheet, one for each student.

✓ **Trading Traits** worksheet, one for each student.

REVIEW:

✓ **Self-Esteem and Body Image Terms *Teacher Background Information*.**

Procedure

■ Explain to students that we will be discussing a topic that affects all of us—*body image*. It is a very personal topic for most people. Therefore, we must remind ourselves of how important it is to be sensitive to the feelings of others during these lessons.

Hand out the **What's Perfect?** worksheet and explain the directions. Students should complete Part I—a description of the perfect body from the point of view of their own gender. Tell students that they will ***not*** be sharing this description with others. It is for their own personal use.

When students have completed the description, lead a discussion of the things that influence body image. Ask students what kinds of things influence how we define a *perfect* body. Responses may include the following:

- media—television, movies, videos, magazines, newspapers
- friends and peer groups
- parents
- what we see in the mirror
- music and television stars

Ask students how the media influence our perceptions and attitudes about body image. Discuss the role of television, movies and videos.

Models, actors and others featured in the media often are slim, with well-proportioned, well-defined figures. Overweight people are seldom featured as models. Heavier than average people are frequently depicted as comical figures in the media.

Discuss billboard, magazine and newspaper advertisements that picture the use of drugs such as tobacco and alcohol as enjoyable.

These ads also use attractive, well-proportioned, slim models. These advertisements often show men and women having fun together. They imply that use of the featured drug will attract others. The product is usually used in an exciting or beautiful setting.

Ask students how these ads influence body image. Point out that many of the products (cigarettes, alcoholic beverages) are used in ads that are specific to a certain gender, culture or ethnic group. Ask students for examples of such advertisements.

Lead students to conclude that media messages seem to say that a slim and muscular body defines *attractive* for both men and women. Emphasize that although it is often a media message, it is not necessary to be slim and muscular to be healthy.

Have students complete Part II of the **What's Perfect?** worksheet. Students should use information from the class discussion to help them identify for themselves the things that influence their attitudes about body image. Tell students to keep this work confidential.

■ Ask students to define *self-esteem.* Share the two definitions in ***Teacher Background Information.*** Then ask students to define *body image.* Use ***Teacher Background Information*** as a guide to class discussion of these terms. Then ask students how self-esteem and body image are related to each other. Ask students how the media message can have an influence on self-esteem.

■ Distribute the **Trading Traits** worksheet. Tell students that to develop high self-esteem and a good self-concept, we must make a realistic assessment of our personal traits. Many people don't recognize their positive qualities, but see only their negative traits.

We need to consider both our positive and negative traits. Then we can decide to work on changing traits that we consider negative.

Tell students that this activity can help them recognize the following points about themselves:

- Who you are.
- How you see yourself.
- How others see you.
- Others do not always see you as you see yourself.
- Everyone has positive and negative points.
- You may be able to change negative traits if you desire.

Emphasize that having a positive self- and body image is *not* conceit. Students should make a realistic and healthful appraisal of themselves without bragging or putting themselves down. In turn, an honest assessment of a partner's traits should not be a put-down or hurtful, but a fair, practical and sensitive evaluation. These assessments can help students understand and evaluate their personal characteristics.

Tell students to choose a partner with whom they feel comfortable. Have students begin by evaluating themselves for each of the traits on the worksheet. When both partners have completed the personal evaluation, have students fold the list back vertically (on the dotted line) and exchange worksheets. *Note:* If a student cannot find a partner with whom he or she feels comfortable sharing this information, the teacher can serve as the partner.

Then each partner should evaluate the other on the list of characteristics. Give students ten to fifteen minutes to make their judgments.

Then ask students to return the lists to their partners. Have students compare what they marked about themselves with what their partners marked. Students will probably see many differences between their self-impressions and how they are perceived by others.

Ask students to review their lists and mark each personal trait (e.g., *sensitive, arrogant*) as a positive or negative trait. Tell them to mark a plus (+) for positive or minus (-) for negative next to the number of the personal trait.

Then ask students to volunteer responses to the following questions:

- Is the image you have of yourself the same image your partner has of you?
- Are there some traits others feel you possess but you do not feel you possess?
- Why are your perceptions different from your partner's?
- If you weren't you, would you like you?
- Do you think you have more negative or positive traits? Why?

Tell students that everyone has traits they do not like. Ask them to think about two of their negative traits. Ask if they agreed with their partner about these traits. Ask how students might try to change negative traits.

Emphasize that we all need to have a sense of perspective about our personal traits. Some things we may be able to change, others we may have to learn to accept.

Remind students that everyone has negative qualities as well as positive ones. Explain that if you think about your friends, you can probably identify a few negative traits in all of them. But you don't let these traits prevent you from continuing the friendship.

Tell students that we should apply these same standards to ourselves. *Like* yourself! Keep your good qualities in sight and remember your strengths and accomplishments when assessing the qualities you might want to change.

Evaluation

Have students write a definition of *body image,* identifying the things that influence their attitudes about body image.

Have students use the information on the **Trading Traits** worksheet to write an essay on three things they learned about themselves during this activity.

Self-Esteem and Body Image Terms

Teacher Background Information

Self-esteem: The judgment a person makes and usually maintains with regard to him- or herself. It expresses an attitude of approval or disapproval and indicates the extent to which a person believes him- or herself capable, significant, successful and worthy (Laing and Breuss, 1989). Self-esteem includes feelings of self-worth and the judgments we make about ourselves, both positive and negative.

The California Task Force to Promote Self-Esteem and Personal and Social Responsibility defined self-esteem as "appreciating my own worth and importance and having the character to be accountable for myself and to act responsibly toward others" (1990).

Body image: Recognition of what the individual is, physically and biologically, with all the changes in the body, is a prerequisite for developing a mature personal identity. The development of a body image and identity acceptable to the adolescent may be affected by current cultural stereotypes of masculinity and femininity. Body image also involves "measuring oneself against others" (Committee on Adolescence, 1968).

Dysmorphophobia: An obsession with a body flaw, blowing it out of proportion.

Personal characteristics: Those traits or characteristics that make up the individual. They include physical, mental-emotional, social and personality traits. Personal characteristics change during adolescence and early adulthood.

Physical traits: Characteristics that relate to appearance. They are visible signs. Changes in physical characteristics during adolescence include growth spurts, development of sex glands and appearance of secondary sex characteristics. These changes are accompanied by the desire to look normal, acceptable and pleasing to self and others.

Mental-emotional traits: Characteristics that relate to feelings, perceptions, experiences, personal relationships, inner conflicts, sexuality, impulses, moodiness and coping mechanisms.

Personality traits: Attitudes, habits, emotions and thoughts that produce a characteristic way of behaving.

Social traits: Characteristics that provide the individual with a sense of self and others. Social characteristics include goal setting, sense of peer group affiliation, building relationships and practicing interpersonal skills.

Mental health: The capacity to cope with life situations, grow emotionally through them, develop to the fullest potential and grow in awareness and consciousness. Mental health is feeling good about oneself, accepting physical appearance, being content with life and gaining inner peace. It is also the active seeking of experiences that promote peak mental states (Laing and Breuss, 1989).

Self-concept: Refers to what the individual thinks, feels and believes about him- or herself. It is her or his understanding of personal abilities, values and feelings.

Anorexia: Loss of appetite. A term incorrectly used to describe individuals with Anorexia Nervosa, since loss of appetite is rare among these individuals.

Anorexia Nervosa: Self starvation associated with emotional, maladaptive behavior; an eating disorder characterized by a psychological condition with progressive weight loss, fear of weight gain, a cycle of repeated ritualistic rigid behavior focused on food, and a distorted body image that can lead to death.

Bulimia: An eating disorder characterized by recurrent episodes of binge eating and secretive purging, using self-induced vomiting, abuse of laxatives and diuretics, fasting and overexercising.

STUDENT

What's Perfect?

Directions: Write a short paragraph about your idea of a "perfect" body. If you are a male, write about a perfect male body. If you are a female, write about a perfect female body. Keep your ideas to yourself. Complete Part II after your class discussion.

Part I

A perfect body is...

Part II

Some of the things that influence this view of perfect are...

STUDENT

Trading Traits

Directions: Look at each of the traits or characteristics on the following list. Think about how each trait applies to you. Circle the letter that indicates how much you are like each of these traits, using the following scale.

SCALE: N = Never; I am not at all like this.
S = Sometimes; this sometimes describes me.
A = Always; I am always like this.

Then fold the paper back on the dotted line to conceal your answer and trade with your partner. Use the same scale to evaluate how each trait applies to your partner.

Traits	Partner	Self	+/–
1. Sensitive	**N S A**	**N S A**	
2. Arrogant	**N S A**	**N S A**	
3. Selfish	**N S A**	**N S A**	
4. Trusting	**N S A**	**N S A**	
5. Caring	**N S A**	**N S A**	
6. Two-faced	**N S A**	**N S A**	
7. Responsible	**N S A**	**N S A**	
8. Funny	**N S A**	**N S A**	
9. Aggressive	**N S A**	**N S A**	
10. Athletic	**N S A**	**N S A**	
11. Beautiful/Handsome	**N S A**	**N S A**	
12. Sarcastic	**N S A**	**N S A**	
13. Attractive	**N S A**	**N S A**	
14. Physically fit	**N S A**	**N S A**	

Traits	Partner	Self	+/–
15. Happy	N S A	N S A	
16. Sad or Depressed	N S A	N S A	
17. Enthusiastic	N S A	N S A	
18. Energetic	N S A	N S A	
19. Social	N S A	N S A	
20. Mature	N S A	N S A	
21. Confident	N S A	N S A	
22. Honest	N S A	N S A	
23. Critical	N S A	N S A	
24. Perfectionist	N S A	N S A	
25. Controlling	N S A	N S A	
26. Anxious	N S A	N S A	
27. Smart	N S A	N S A	
28. Productive	N S A	N S A	
29. Self-centered	N S A	N S A	
30. Successful	N S A	N S A	
31. Sincere	N S A	N S A	
32. Goal-oriented	N S A	N S A	

Adapted from Rosa Sullivan. 1984. The mirror game. *Health education teaching ideas: Secondary.* Ed. R. Loya. Reston, VA: American Alliance for Health, Physical Education, Recreation and Dance.

LESSON 2

PRESSURES ON BODY IMAGE

Objectives

Students will be able to evaluate body image messages in advertising.

Students will be able to list realistic ways to improve body image.

Time

One class period.

Overview

Social, cultural and historical beliefs about body image influence our present-day perceptions about our physical selves. The mass media, parents and peers probably have the most influence on students.

In this lesson, students look at pressure and influences on body image. They analyze advertisements for their influence on body image. As homework, they complete an assessment that measures their self-esteem about body image.

Teacher Materials and Preparation

ASSIGN:

✓ Students to look in magazines and newspapers and cut out advertisements that they think contain a message about body image. Advertisements will be for a variety of products, including clothing, cigarettes, alcoholic beverages, weight control products, etc. Students should bring these advertisements to this class.

HAVE:

✓ Overhead projector (optional).

✓ Blank transparencies *or* butcher paper, one piece for each group of four or five students (optional).

✓ Transparency marker *or* colored markers (optional).

✓ Chalk and chalkboard.

COPY:

✓ **Body Image Pressures** student information sheet, one for each student.

✓ **Survival Notes** student information sheet, one for each student.

✓ **Media Messages** worksheet, two for each student.

✓ **Looking at Myself** worksheet, one for each student.

REVIEW:

✓ **Culture and Body Image *Teacher Background Information*.**

Procedure

■ Ask students to recall the definition of body image discussed in Lesson 1. *Body image* refers to the view we have of our physical selves. Developing a positive body image can help us see ourselves as attractive people.

Tell students that exploration, experimentation, communication and learning about ourselves can help us develop a positive body image. As we discover our personal strengths and weaknesses, we must learn to like ourselves in spite of our limitations.

The way we feel about our physical selves affects our self-esteem (the judgments we make about our personal competence). It also has an important effect on our overall behavior.

Tell students that people with positive body images usually have wholesome and positive attitudes about other aspects of themselves. Our personal level of wellness is affected by the ways we think about and value ourselves. We can be healthier if we like ourselves and think about ourselves in positive terms.

Explain that skin texture, complexion and teeth contribute in important ways to our physical appearance. Grooming and personal hygiene (cleanliness, make-up, hairstyle) also have an effect. However, there are four other factors that affect physical appearance. They are:

- the dimensions (length and breadth) of the skeletal framework
- the distribution and development of the muscles resting upon the skeleton
- the amount and location of adipose tissue (fat) throughout the body
- the clothing that covers the body

These factors account for most of the physical image we project. Point out that the first factor—the basic body framework—is a function of heredity and genetics (for better or worse). We may be able to control or influence the latter three factors, although heredity and genetics also play a role in the development of muscle mass and fat.

■ Tell students that pressures around ideal body images can lead to eating disorders. Distribute the **Body Image Pressures** student information sheet, and ask students to read it.

When students have finished reading, lead a class discussion of the pressures on both males and females to meet certain standards for physical appearance. Include the following questions:

- What are some of the pressures on boys around body image? on girls?
- How are the pressures different for boys and girls?
- How are they alike?
- What are some of the differences in the ways boys and girls cope with these pressures?

■ Then ask students to think about other ways our society and our culture pressure people to change or dislike their bodies and body image. Use **Culture and Body Image** ***Teacher Background Information*** to guide this discussion.

Emphasize that individuals cannot change their basic body structure. We may not have the build of a fashion model, gymnast or body builder, but whatever body type we have, we can be fit.

■ Ask students: How can we improve body image? Divide the class into small groups, and distribute the **Survival Notes** student information sheet. Tell students to discuss the information in their groups. Ask groups to list other ideas on the chalkboard or butcher paper or an overhead transparency and report to the class.

You may want to include these additional suggestions:

- Look into a mirror. Note your positive features and think about how they can be enhanced.
- Look closely at the features or body parts you consider least attractive.
- Put up photographs of yourself that you like.
- The next time you go to extra effort to look good, say aloud to the mirror, "I look great today."
- Pamper yourself with relaxing baths, fragrances, a new haircut, new clothes or accessories.
- Ask friends and family members what they find physically attractive about you.
- Work on your physical potential with exercise and healthy eating.
- Talk with other people if you feel lonely or isolated.
- Keep a mental list of the positive ways you've grown and improved.

■ Ask students to take out the advertisements with body image messages. Distribute the **Media Messages** worksheet. Review the directions with students. Tell students to use the worksheet to evaluate their advertisements. Note that the higher the advertisement scores, the more likely it is to affect body image.

When students have completed the worksheet, ask them to report on the messages in the advertisements. Discuss whether these messages have a positive or negative effect on personal body image. Then ask students to share their final ratings from Step III and Step IV of the worksheet. How could the advertisements be changed to make them more accurate?

Evaluation

Have students use the **Media Messages** worksheet to evaluate an advertisement on television. Tell students to complete the form, then comment in writing on how television differs from printed media. You may also want to suggest that students talk to a parent or other trusted adult about the criteria the media use to assess body image.

Have students write a list of things that individuals can do to improve their body image. Suggest that students list only things that can be done in a short time frame. These steps should be realistic ones that could be accomplished within a few days.

Homework

Distribute the **Looking at Myself** worksheet for students to complete as homework. Discuss the directions. Tell students to complete the assessment, then add up all the point values they assigned to the parts of the body and divide the sum by 40. Scores should fall between 1 and 5.

Tell students this scale measures self-esteem about body image, or how well you like your body. What you think of your body and what you think of yourself are very important to your self-esteem.

If you are dissatisfied with parts of your body or other aspects of yourself, think about whether they are things you can change. What changes can you make? If there are things you can't change, how can you learn to be more accepting of them?

Suggest that if students are dissatisfied with energy level, appetite, exercise level or rate, body build, weight, health or posture, they may be able to design a fitness or personal grooming and hygiene program to improve those areas.

Follow-Up/ Extension

Suggest that students write letters to the advertising and/or manufacturing companies of advertised products to suggest ways that body image may be portrayed more realistically.

Culture and Body Image

Teacher Background Information

Culture refers to the knowledge, traditions, beliefs and values that are developed, learned and shared by members of a society. Shared norms, beliefs and values are part of a group's culture and influence individual thoughts and decisions we make about ourselves, our families and society.

While culture is a useful concept for describing a group in general terms, there is much intracultural variation. People from the same culture may have very different diets, eating behaviors and perceptions of desirable body weight for individuals and groups.

Slenderness has become a major preoccupation for many North Americans. The diet industry is now a multimillion-dollar business as people turn to diet pills, sodas, drinks and other potions in their quest for thinness. Weight-loss books are best sellers. Exercise spas and weight-loss clinics, clubs and enrollment programs are a booming business.

Definitions of the ideal body size and shape vary from one culture to another. North Americans consider a slim figure both attractive and healthy; success is associated with slimness. Overweight people frequently face discrimination from employers and others who unfairly assume that they are lazy, messy and lack character or self-restraint.

The slim, attractive female is a pervasive image in our culture. The ideal male image is usually an athletic-looking body, lean and tall with well-defined musculature. Movie stars, television personalities, fashion models and advertisements all reflect these images.

Our culture is not the only one that promotes a thin body image. Over the centuries, it has been documented that the Cretans, Athenians, Spartans and others were concerned about body fat.

Obesity, in contrast, is the ideal body image for many cultures. Fat is a sign of wealth, and the luxury of inactivity and overeating is a sign of good health. Polynesians, Samoans and past European societies have admired the obese.

Cultural definitions of ideal body types change through time. During the 1920s, in the United States, the flapper was a lean, flat-chested, angular-looking female. Thirty years later, Marilyn Monroe replaced that look with the no-bones look—a more voluptuous, softer, rounder figure.

In the 1920s the average woman was 5'3" tall and weighed approximately 120 pounds; now the average woman is 5'5" and weighs 128 pounds. The average male is about fifteen pounds heavier now.

In the 1980s the typical Miss America was between 5'6" and 5'11" tall and weighed between 110-120 pounds. She exercised an average of 14 hours per week and had small hips and large breasts (almost a physical impossibility for that height and weight).

In the 1980s, Jane Fonda's slim, toned body type became the rage. However, magazines and journals reported that Jane Fonda had an eating disorder, bulimia, that affected her for 20 years.

Many people in our society are not only obsessed with weight, but with other body imperfections. Movie stars and others submit to cosmetic surgery in an attempt to obtain a flawless appearance. Nose jobs, liposuction, tummy and buttocks tucks and rib removal are commonly used in the search for the perfect body.

Eating disorders, especially anorexia nervosa and bulimia, affect 10 to 15 percent of adolescent girls. Those affected are mostly White and middle to upper class; only a few cases of Black adolescents with these disorders have been reported. However, it is likely that these disorders are underreported for Blacks and other racial and ethnic groups.

Eating disorders may also be underreported in adolescent males. Some adolescent males resort to steroid use and body building in efforts to achieve the masculine ideal.

Sometimes at this stage of development, adolescent males do not like to perceive themselves as small or thin. They may not be able to be as involved in sports, and girls may be taller than they are. These issues are important to most male adolescents.

Surveys have indicated that as many as 70 percent of high school girls are unhappy with their bodies and want to lose weight. Even among female adolescents of normal weight range for their height and gender, as many as 83 percent want to lose weight.

Methods of weight loss used by these females include diet pills, fasting and crash diets. Sources of information about weight control and dieting tend to be the mass media, family members and athletic coaches. Teachers and the school nurse are rarely used.

When a normal weight or thin individual diets for weight control purposes, she or he may have a disturbed body image. The term for fixating on a body flaw and blowing it out of proportion is *dysmorphophobia*.

In some cases, cultural images of ideal body size and the methods used to achieve them have serious health consequences. Research has shown that both very thin and very fat people have increased rates of disease and early death.

Physical and physiological body changes associated with adolescence vary in relation to the sociocultural environment. For example, there is a vast difference in the age of menarche in different cultures and within subcultures.

Nutritional or health-care differences associated with various sociocultural settings might account for the age differences. Scarcity of nutritional resources may delay menarche (females who have many siblings may have less to eat, which may delay menarche). Tropical and warm environments (heat and humidity are related to early menarche) may also have an effect on maturation. Historically, females in the United States in the 1890s had menarche at about fourteen to fifteen years of age; today, however, they reach this point at about age twelve.

The Weight Controversy

Medically, ideal or desirable weight is usually determined in terms of height. Because relative amounts of fat, lean (muscle) tissue and bone size vary greatly from person to person, ideal weights are given as ranges in recommended weight tables. For example, recommended weight for a 5'4" woman with a medium frame is between 124 and 138 pounds.

Some experts have challenged the recommended weight tables. They suggest that the concept of ideal weight should be more flexible. Health hazards are associated only with extreme overweight and underweight (20 percent over or under ideal range). These experts suggest that efforts to change body weight should focus on these people, rather than on those whose weights deviate only minimally from the ideal.

It is important to be sure that this percentage of weight over the average is contributed by an excess of body fat and not body muscle (muscle weighs four times more than body fat). A weight lifter might be heavier than average, but this excess weight is due to more body muscle than average; therefore, the weight lifter would not be considered obese.

for your information

Body Image Pressures

From early childhood, our society teaches us that appearance is very important. Feeling attractive is an essential part of self-worth. Children quickly learn that others will judge us by how we look. Success seems to be promised to those whose looks match a certain ideal.

For women, this ideal is a tall, thin, young, well-proportioned body. The male is tall with an athletic-looking body, well-defined muscles and no evident fat. Both male and female ideals have flawless complexions and beautiful teeth as shown in television, movies, magazines, newspapers and billboards.

Most of us will never look like this. But the message we get is that we can meet this ideal if we try hard enough. When we believe this message, we can become very unhappy. We may spend many hours and a lot of money trying to change our appearance.

When we fail to achieve these impossible standards, we may feel incompetent, have low self-esteem and be depressed. Many researchers believe that anorexia nervosa and bulimia can result from attempts to attain society's ideals.

These eating disorders can be a problem both for males and females. Although more women than men have an eating disorder, at least one of every ten individuals with an eating disorder is male, usually between the ages of thirteen and 30.

Men and women need to develop personal skills that help them feel good about themselves. They should not rely on dieting, exercise and dressing a certain way to attain a successful look. Many messages about body image suggest that to be successful, appearance is as important as ability. According to these messages, it is not enough to simply be good at what you do.

When we understand these body image messages, we can develop the skills to deal with them.

+ SURVIVAL NOTES +

DO:

Accept that bodies come in a variety of shapes and sizes—and this makes life interesting.

Remember that you can be your worst critic. Others may find you really attractive.

Expect normal weekly and monthly changes in weight and shape.

Explore your internal self—emotionally, spiritually and as a growing, changing human being.

Explore all the things you have to offer others—caring, enthusiasm, information, company, love and honesty.

Decide how you wish to spend your energy—pursuing the perfect image or enjoying family, friends and school.

Be aware of your own weight prejudice. Explore how those feelings may affect your self-esteem.

DON'T:

...Let your body define who or what you are. You are much more than just a body.

...Let obsession with your body keep you from getting close to others or taking risks.

...Judge others on the basis of appearance, body size or shape.

...Forget that society changes its idea of beauty over the years.

...Believe that all thin people are happy with themselves.

...Forget that you are not alone in your pursuit of self-acceptance. It is a lifelong process that many people struggle with.

...Be afraid to actually enjoy your body. It doesn't have to be something you are *stuck* with.

Media Messages

Directions: Answer the following questions about an advertisement. Then complete the *Scoring and Interpretation* section, following *Steps I-IV.*

What is the name of the advertised product? ______________________________

What kind of product is it? Circle or fill in the blank space below.

Diet (weight control)	Alcoholic beverage (beer, wine, liquor)
Clothing	Other ____________________
Tobacco product	

Rate the advertisement on each of the following factors, using this scale:

SA = Strongly Agree	D = Disagree
A = Agree	SD = Strongly Disagree
U = Undecided	NA = Not Applicable

Circle *one* choice for each statement.

Generally, the advertisement:		**Score**
1. Suggests that use of the product will produce a positive body image.	**SA A U D SD NA**	______
2. Shows a socially negative body image.	**SA A U D SD NA**	______
3. Suggests the product is a solution for boredom.	**SA A U D SD NA**	______
4. Associates the use of the product with fun or pleasure.	**SA A U D SD NA**	______
5. Associates the use of the product with being attractive.	**SA A U D SD NA**	______
6. Encourages the use of the product as a method of problem-solving.	**SA A U D SD NA**	______
7. Suggests that everyone is using the product.	**SA A U D SD NA**	______
8. Suggests that people who use the product are mature.	**SA A U D SD NA**	______
9. Shows the model using the product.	**SA A U D SD NA**	______
10. Suggests that the product will improve performance (intellectual, physical, spiritual, etc.).	**SA A U D SD NA**	______
	Total:	______

Scoring and Interpretation of Results

Step I. Use the following scale to score your responses.

[SA] Strongly Agree = 5 points
[A] Agree = 4 points
[U] Undecided = 3 points
[D] Disagree = 2 points
[SD] Strongly Disagree = 1 point
[NA] Not Applicable = 0 points

Step II. Add your points for each statement:

Total Points: _______Points

Step III. After you have added up the total points, place an X on the point of the following line that best represents your total points.

Total Points

10 **20** **30** **40** **50**

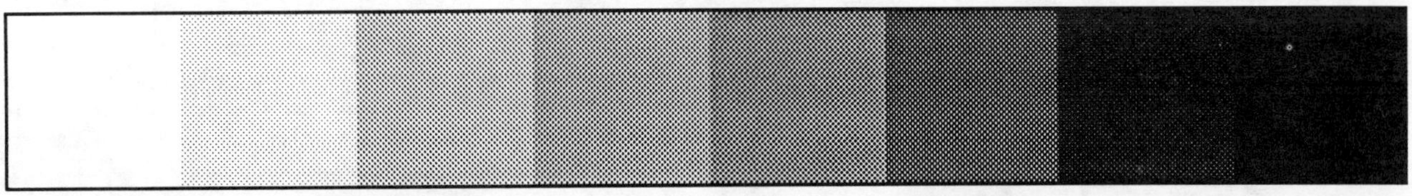

Little Impact on Body Image **High Impact on Body Image**

Step IV. Write your comments regarding your analysis or evaluation of the body image in the advertisement. (e.g., What decisions did you reach about the body image?)

____

____

____

____

____

____

____

STUDENT

Looking at Myself

Directions: Using the scale below, place the number next to each body part or other characteristic listed that describes your feeling about that part of yourself.

Scale:

1. I have strong feelings and wish I could change this.
2. I don't like this, but I can put up with this.
3. I have no particular feelings about this.
4. I am satisfied with this.
5. I consider myself fortunate with this.

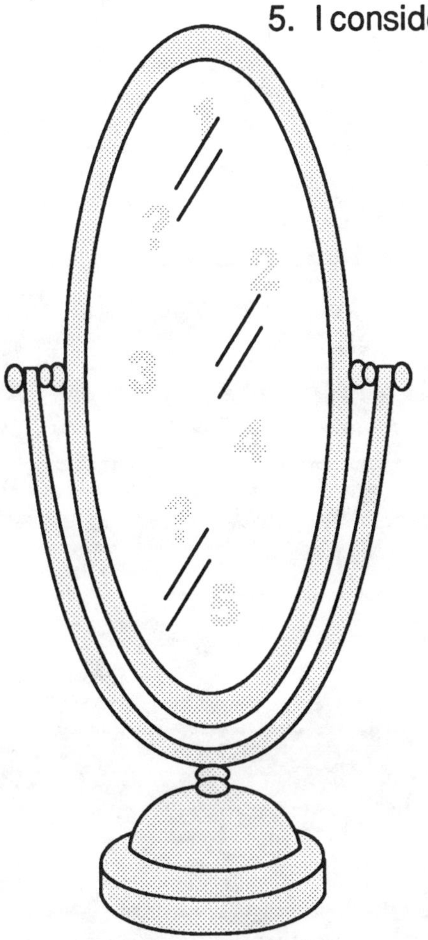

_____ 1. hair
_____ 2. facial complexion
_____ 3. appetite
_____ 4. hands
_____ 5. distribution of body hair
_____ 6. nose
_____ 7. fingers
_____ 8. wrists
_____ 9. waist
_____ 10. energy level
_____ 11. back
_____ 12. ears
_____ 13. chin
_____ 14. exercise
_____ 15. ankles
_____ 16. neck
_____ 17. head shape
_____ 18. body build
_____ 19. profile
_____ 20. height
_____ 21. weight
_____ 22. age
_____ 23. shoulder width
_____ 24. arms
_____ 25. chest
_____ 26. eyes
_____ 27. digestion
_____ 28. hips
_____ 29. lips
_____ 30. legs
_____ 31. teeth
_____ 32. forehead
_____ 33. feet
_____ 34. voice
_____ 35. health
_____ 36. knees
_____ 37. posture
_____ 38. face
_____ 39. fingernails
_____ 40. eyelashes

Scoring: Add up all the point values you assigned to the characteristics and divide the sum by 40. Your score should fall between 1 and 5.

A score closer to 5 indicates you are very comfortable with your body image. A score closer to 1 indicates that you are very uncomfortable. You may need to think about changing your attitude to improve your self-esteem about your body image. You may also want to consider healthful ways to change your appearance.

LESSON 3

EATING DISORDERS

Objectives

Students will be able to identify the characteristics of anorexia nervosa and bulimia.

Students will be able to explain the relationship between eating disorders and body image.

Time

Two class periods.

Overview

Many Americans believe that thinner is better. People with eating disorders believe it so deeply that their weight and dieting success become the measure of their self-image and self-esteem. Because they think eating is both the cause and result of many of their problems, these people become trapped in a cycle of repeated, ritualistic and rigid behavior focused on food.

In this lesson, students examine eating disorders and prepare class presentations. They also work in groups to create collages that represent factors that influence eating disorders. Pre- and post-tests help students assess their learning.

Teacher Materials and Preparation

HAVE:

✓ Contemporary magazines.
✓ Scissors, glue and colored markers.
✓ Overhead projector (optional).
✓ Blank transparencies *or* butcher paper, four pieces (optional).
✓ Transparency marker (optional).
✓ Posterboard, one piece for each group.

COPY:

✓ **Check Your Knowledge** worksheet, two for each student.
✓ **What Causes Eating Disorders?** student information sheet, for one-fourth of the class.
✓ **What Is Anorexia Nervosa?** student information sheet, for one-fourth of the class.
✓ **What Is Bulimia?** student information sheet, for one-fourth of the class.
✓ **Drugs and Eating Disorders** student information sheet, for one-fourth of the class.

REVIEW:

✓ **Symptoms of Eating Disorders** ***Teacher Background Information.***
✓ **Check Your Knowledge** ***Key.***

Procedure

■ Distribute the **Check Your Knowledge** worksheet. Tell students the worksheet will measure how much they know about eating disorders. At the end of this lesson, they will take the survey again to see how much they've learned.

■ When students have completed the worksheet, divide the class into four groups. Distribute a different student information sheet to each group (causes of eating disorders, anorexia nervosa, bulimia or drugs). Tell students to read and discuss the topic with their group.

Have each group prepare a class presentation on their topic. Encourage students to use blank transparencies or butcher paper to make lists of symptoms and other important points to use during the presentations.

After the group presentations, lead a class discussion of eating disorders. Use **Symptoms of Eating Disorders *Teacher Background Information*** as a resource for this discussion.

■ Divide class into groups of four or five students each. Distribute one piece of posterboard to each group, with scissors, glue, tape and colored markers. Tell students to use pictures from magazines or their own drawings to develop a collage that represents factors that influence body image and eating disorders.

Tell students to label the factors as they relate to the characteristics associated with the eating disorders discussed in class. Have groups present their collages to the class, explaining the images and factors they used. Post the collages in the classroom.

Evaluation

Distribute another copy of the **Check Your Knowledge** worksheet. Have students complete it, then review the correct answers, using the **Check Your Knowledge *Key*** as a guide. Have students write a paragraph comparing their scores on the pre- and post-tests.

Have students write a paragraph that answers the following question: How are eating disorders related to body image? Assess students' ability to describe the relationship between eating disorders and body image.

Follow-Up/ Extension

Have students read stories and books about people with eating disorders and their experiences, including Karen Carpenter, Cherry Boone, Jane Fonda, Cathy Rigby, etc.

Symptoms of Eating Disorders

Teacher Background Information

Anorexia nervosa and bulimia are the most serious eating disorders afflicting today's teenagers. Anorexia nervosa is characterized by a distorted body image and intense fear of gaining weight or becoming fat. People with anorexia nervosa may insist that they are fat even when they are obviously underweight. Anorexia nervosa leads to severe, life-threatening weight loss.

Bulimia is characterized by recurrent episodes of bingeing and purging. In bulimia, weight changes are usually not life-threatening, although people with anorexia nervosa may also have bulimic episodes.

Complications of Anorexia Nervosa and Bulimia

Some of the problems and complications of anorexia nervosa and bulimia include:

The esophagus (the tube connecting the mouth and stomach) can be injured by repeated vomiting. Acid from the stomach irritates and inflames the membrane that lines the esophagus. This esophagitis is sometimes severe enough to cause scarring and narrowing. The passageway becomes so narrow that it is difficult for food to pass through.

The physical stress of vomiting can cause tears in the lining of the esophagus, causing massive bleeding, or the esophagus may rupture. These problems can be life-threatening.

Binge eating may cause injury to the stomach. Frequent vomiting commonly causes gastritis, an inflammation of the stomach lining. On very rare occasions, eating a large meal very rapidly, combined with slower emptying of food from the stomach, may cause the stomach to rupture, causing death from peritonitis.

Injury to the intestines, particularly the colon, commonly results from laxative abuse. Damage to the lining may lead to ulcers and produce bloody stools.

Lung complications occur when self-induced vomiting leads to aspiration of food particles, gastric acid and bacteria. These substances move from the stomach into the lungs and may cause pneumonia.

Kidney and heart complications are often severe. Fasting, vomiting and other forms of purging result in loss of fluid and crucial minerals from the body. Chronic dehydration and low potassium levels can lead to kidney stones and even kidney failure. Loss of body acids as a result of frequent vomiting leads to high alkali levels in the blood and body tissues. This may cause weakness, constipation and tiredness. Severe alkalosis and potassium deficiency can lead to an uneven heart rate or sudden death.

Injury to the skin occurs in various ways. Most over-the-counter laxatives contain phenolphthalein, which may cause sores in the skin and hyperpigmentation (brown or gray spots).

Excessive and forceful vomiting may result in hemorrhages in the blood vessels of the eye, fluid retention and swelling of the parotid glands, causing chipmunk cheeks.

Injury to the teeth is quite common. Chronic vomiting increases the acidity of the mouth and results in erosion of the tooth enamel and dentin.

A Multidimensional Profile

Anorexia Nervosa	*Bulimia*
Early Symptoms • low self-esteem • misperception of hunger, fullness and other bodily sensations • feelings of lack of control in life • distorted body image • overachiever • compliant • anxious	**Early Symptoms** • low self-esteem • feeling that self-worth is dependent on low weight • dependent on opposite sex for approval • normal weight • constant concern with weight and body image • experimentation with vomiting, laxatives and diuretics • poor impulse control • fear that bingeing and eating are getting out of control
Middle Stage Symptoms • menstrual cycle stops (amenorrhea) with extreme weight loss • increasing preoccupation with food and eating • isolates self from family and friends • perfectionistic behavior • compulsive exercise • eats alone • fights with family • attempts to control family's eating • increased amount of facial and body hair (lanugo) • fatigue • decreased amount of scalp hair and thin, dry scalp	**Middle Stage Symptoms** • embarrassment • anxiety • depression • self-indulgent behavior • eats alone • preoccupied with eating and food • tiredness, apathy, irritability • gastrointestinal disorders • anemia • social isolation, distancing friends and family • dishonesty, lying, stealing food or money • tooth damage (gum disease) • "chipmunk" (puffy) cheeks • drug and alcohol abuse • laxative and diuretic abuse

Crucial Stage Symptoms

- emaciated appearance (at least 25 percent loss of total body weight)
- feelings of control over body
- rigid
- depression and apathy
- fear of food and gaining weight
- malnutrition
- mood swings
- diminished capacity to think
- sensitivity to cold
- electrolyte imbalance (weakness)
- denial of problem (sees self as fat)
- joint pain (difficulty walking and sitting)
- sleep disturbance

Crucial Stage Symptoms

- mood swings
- chronic sore throat
- difficulties in breathing or swallowing
- hypokalemia (abnormally low potassium concentration)
- electrolyte imbalance
- general ill health, constant physical problems
- possible rupture of heart or esophagus, peritonitis
- dehydration
- irregular heart rhythms
- suicidal tendencies

Recognition of Need for Help

Rehabilitation

- acceptance of a psychiatric treatment plan
- participation in a treatment program that includes the family
- acceptance of illness
- resumption of normal self-control and normal eating
- diminished fears
- relief from guilt and depression
- achievement of personal goals in a wide range of activities
- new friends, new interests
- return of regular menstrual cycles
- acceptance of personal limitations
- more understanding of family
- developing optimism
- improved self-image
- increased assertiveness
- honesty
- understanding of personal needs
- trust and openness

Recovery

Ongoing Support (with family)

---

for your information

What Causes Eating Disorders?

Many teenagers believe that dieting is the normal way to eat. Every magazine, billboard, movie, television show and commercial seems to send a message that happiness is being thin. According to these messages, being thin also leads to success, self-confidence and respect.

People with eating disorders believe these messages. They spend much of their time and energy thinking about what they eat and how they look. They focus on their appearance and don't develop their confidence and abilities in other areas.

Psychological Factors
People who have eating disorders work hard to prove that they are good enough, because they're afraid they aren't. They are competitive and ambitious. They want to be perfect. They seem to think: If I am thin, I will be happy, popular, successful and self-confident.

Family Problems
Teens with eating disorders may be afraid to grow up and leave the safety of school and their families. Some teens use eating disorders as an excuse to remain dependent on their parents. Others use their unusual food behaviors as a way to assert their independence and rebel against family standards.

An eating disorder can be a symbolic protest against parents who the teen may think are too strict. In some families, the teen feels he or she has to take care of the parents, and does not want this unfair responsibility.

Lifestyle Factors
People with eating disorders may not be very assertive. They usually don't handle stress well. They don't have important goals that can help them feel independent and self-confident. They may have friends who are also very concerned about physical appearance and thinness. Some occupations or careers are associated with an extreme emphasis on appearance and/or weight control. Many dancers, actresses, models, gymnasts, flight attendants, sorority members and jockeys have eating disorders.

Biological Factors
There may be biological reasons that make some people more likely than others to develop an eating disorder. They may be related to people who are alcoholic or depressed or both. People with certain types of eating disorders may also abuse alcohol and other drugs.

Dieting or limiting your eating over a long period of time can cause the body processes to be out of balance. These changes in the body can lead to eating disorders. Most of the physical problems are results, not causes, of eating disorders.

(continued)

Poor nutrition causes changes in the way the body uses calories from food. These changes make it hard to lose weight and easy to gain. The frustration this causes can lead people to overeat (binge), then try to get rid of the food by vomiting (purging). These behaviors can make the problem even worse.

Triggers

Many of the factors that contribute to eating disorders can exist for years before anything happens. Then something may set off a cycle of strict dieting or bingeing and purging. The event that sets off this cycle is called a *trigger.*

Trigger incidents are problems a person is not prepared to handle. Triggers can include losses such as death, divorce or leaving home; school pressures; a long-distance move; or the break-up of an important relationship. Many teens with eating disorders report that teasing from their peers or other comments about their bodies made them think they were fat and needed to diet.

Many people with eating disorders are also victims of rape, incest, molestation, verbal abuse and neglect. Because they don't know how to express their fear, rage, confusion and need for help, they turn to or away from food. They may use food for comfort, or they may go on strict diets to help them feel in control of something in their lives.

for your information

What Is Anorexia Nervosa?

Anorexia nervosa is an eating disorder that can be a serious problem. People with this disorder say they feel fat or that parts of their bodies are fat, even if they weigh much less than is normal or healthy. They may feel uncomfortable after eating a normal or even a very small meal.

People with anorexia nervosa are very concerned about their body size. They are usually unhappy with some feature of their physical appearance. They spend a lot of time thinking about eating, food, weight and body image.

They may count calories, weigh themselves many times a day and go on strict diets, even if they are very thin. They may think of foods as good or bad. They may also judge how well they control their eating habits.

Such people usually lose weight by reducing the amount of food they eat and exercising a lot. Some people with anorexia nervosa may make themselves vomit or use laxatives or diuretics. They may also have bulimia. At least 40 percent of people with anorexia nervosa also suffer from bulimia.

Other peculiar behaviors concerning food are common. People with anorexia nervosa often fix very special meals for others, but limit themselves to a few low-calorie foods. They may hide food or throw it away.

Some anorexics may feel compelled to wash their hands frequently or behave in other unusual ways. Most people with anorexia nervosa exercise compulsively. They don't believe they have a problem with food or eating.

The problem usually begins in the early to late teens. It occurs most often in females. The beginning of the illness is often related to problems that cause stress.

Many of these teens are described as model children. About one-third of them are slightly overweight before the problem begins. The disorder is more common among people who have sisters and mothers who are anorexic.

Many people have only one episode of anorexia nervosa and then return to normal eating patterns and weight. In other cases, weight loss may be so severe that the victim has to be hospitalized to prevent death by starvation. Studies indicate that between 5 and 18 percent of people with this eating disorder die.

for your information

What Is Bulimia?

Bulimia is an eating disorder characterized by bingeing and purging. Binge eating is eating a large amount of food in a short period of time. Purging refers to trying to get rid of the food that's been eaten by vomiting or using laxatives or diuretics.

People with this disorder may feel they are out of control during the eating binges. They are very concerned about body shape and weight. They may try other ways to prevent weight gain, including diet aids, strict diets, fasts or lots of exercise.

People with bulimia may plan eating binges. They will buy food to eat during the binge which is often sweet and high in calories. It may also be easy to eat quickly, without a lot of chewing, such as ice cream. The binge is usually kept hidden from others. Once the binge has begun, the person may look for more food to eat when the food that started the binge is gone.

A binge usually ends when the binger's stomach starts to hurt or if someone interrupts. After bingeing, the binger may make him- or herself vomit. Vomiting is a form of purging. It reduces the stomach pain. Then the binger may start eating again or end the binge. Sometimes the binge ends with the binger going to sleep.

Although a binge may seem enjoyable at the time, the binger often feels depressed afterwards. Vomiting may reduce some of the guilt associated with bingeing.

The problem usually begins in adolescence or early adult life. People with bulimia may be slightly underweight, but more often they are slightly overweight. Whatever they weigh, they are very concerned about it.

Binges usually alternate with periods of normal eating or with periods of normal eating and fasting. When the problem gets worse, the victim may either binge or fast with no periods of normal eating. A person who has an average of two or more binge-eating episodes a week for at least three months would be considered bulimic.

Weight may change often due to the alternating binges and fasts. Bulimics often feel that their lives are dominated by conflicts about eating. Bulimia seldom interferes with normal activities, except in a few people who spend their entire day binge eating and vomiting. The vomiting may harm teeth and cause chemical imbalance in the body and dehydration. These problems may affect the heart and can cause sudden death.

STUDENT

for your information

Drugs and Eating Disorders

Laxatives seem to move food through the body more rapidly. They may relieve stomach bloating and pain after a binge. However, they don't prevent the calories in food from being absorbed into the body. Any weight loss is due mostly to loss of water and minerals in the bowel movement and is temporary. This weight will naturally be gained back.

Misuse of laxatives is harmful. Some of the harmful effects include:

- They upset the body's mineral balance.
- They lead to dehydration (not enough water in the cells of the body).
- They damage the lining of the digestive tract.
- They let the digestive tract get lazy; someone who uses laxatives regularly may become constipated without them.

Diuretics or water pills increase the amount of urine. They can cause sudden weight loss. But they can also cause dehydration. Diuretics are dangerous, because they can increase the loss of important minerals—calcium, potassium, magnesium and zinc—from the body. In a rebound effect, they can also cause the body to retain salt and water, making it more sensitive to diet changes.

Ipecac syrup is taken to cause vomiting. It is used in an emergency to treat people who have swallowed poison. It has been linked to the deaths of several people with eating disorders. The active ingredient (emetine) can build up in body tissues and cause muscle or heart weakness. Ipecac is toxic (poisonous), whether taken in large amounts or small amounts that build up over time.

Diet pills are often taken to help with weight loss. The best known pills are Dexedrine and Benzedrine. These require a prescription from a doctor. However, the FDA prohibits doctors from prescribing these drugs for weight loss.

Dexatrim, Dietac and Contac are over-the-counter drugs available without a prescription. These drugs are also misused. They temporarily reduce the appetite. Usually, the appetite returns to normal after a week or two, and the lost weight is gained back. Then the user has the problem of trying to get off the drug without gaining more weight.

These drugs don't really help people lose weight and keep it off. They can be dangerously addictive.

Check Your Knowledge

Directions: Read each of the following statements. Circle the letter **T** if the statement is completely true; circle the letter **F** if the statement is partly or completely false.

T **F** 1. Teens may develop unusual eating behaviors as a way to become independent and rebel against authority, such as parents and teachers.

T **F** 2. Eating a lot of food in a short time is called bingeing.

T **F** 3. Insisting that your body is fat, even when you're very thin, is a symptom of anorexia nervosa.

T **F** 4. Being teased by friends about being fat or needing to diet can trigger an eating disorder.

T **F** 5. Thinking about food all the time is a symptom of eating disorders.

T **F** 6. Feeling depressed often is a symptom of eating disorders.

T **F** 7. Losing too much weight due to starvation is a symptom of anorexia nervosa.

T **F** 8. Most weight-loss diets provide normal ways to eat for a lifetime.

T **F** 9. Forcing yourself to vomit is one of the common behaviors of anorexia nervosa.

T **F** 10. Only females are affected by bulimia.

T **F** 11. Diet pills are a good way to help people lose weight and keep it off.

T **F** 12. People can become addicted to diet pills.

T **F** 13. People with eating disorders have low self-esteem.

T **F** 14. Most people with anorexia nervosa deny that their eating behavior is a serious problem.

T **F** 15. People with eating disorders believe that a thin body will bring them happiness and success.

Check Your Knowledge

Key

Directions: Read each of the following statements. Circle the letter **T** if the statement is completely true; circle the letter **F** if the statement is partly or completely false.

(T) F 1. Teens may develop unusual eating behaviors as a way to become independent and rebel against authority, such as parents and teachers.

(T) F 2. Eating a lot of food in a short time is called bingeing.

(T) F 3. Insisting that your body is fat, even when you're very thin, is a symptom of anorexia nervosa.

(T) F 4. Being teased by friends about being fat or needing to diet can trigger an eating disorder.

(T) F 5. Thinking about food all the time is a symptom of eating disorders.

(T) F 6. Feeling depressed often is a symptom of eating disorders.

(T) F 7. Losing too much weight due to starvation is a symptom of anorexia nervosa.

T (F) 8. Most weight-loss diets provide normal ways to eat for a lifetime.

T (F) 9. Forcing yourself to vomit is one of the common behaviors of anorexia nervosa.

T (F) 10. Only females are affected by bulimia.

T (F) 11. Diet pills are a good way to help people lose weight and keep it off.

(T) F 12. People can become addicted to diet pills.

(T) F 13. People with eating disorders have low self-esteem.

(T) F 14. Most people with anorexia nervosa deny that their eating behavior is a serious problem.

(T) F 15. People with eating disorders believe that a thin body will bring them happiness and success.

LESSON 4

HELP FOR EATING DISORDERS

Objectives

Students will be able to illustrate prevention behaviors for eating disorders.

Students will be able to differentiate between normal teen-age eating behaviors and eating disorder behaviors.

Time

One class session.

Overview

The best treatment for eating disorders is prevention. Early detection of a possible problem and prompt, competent treatment are important.

This lesson begins with a worksheet to help students analyze whom they can talk to about possible problems. Students discuss the difference between normal dieting versus eating disorder behaviors for teenagers. The worksheet helps students recognize if they, or someone they know, might have an eating disorder. As a follow-up, students research referral and treatment resources within the community.

Teacher Materials and Preparation

HAVE:

✓ Overhead projector.
✓ Transparency marker.

COPY:

✓ **Privacy Circles** worksheet, one for each student.
✓ **Problems Eating You?** worksheet, one for each student.

MAKE:

✓ Transparency of **Privacy Circles**.
✓ Transparency of **Normal or Not?**.
✓ Transparency of **Prevention Pointers**.
✓ Transparency *or* poster of **Help for Eating Disorders**.

REVIEW:

✓ **Overcoming Eating Disorders *Teacher Background Information*.**
✓ **Treatment of Eating Disorders,** Appendix A.

Procedure

■ Explain to students that an individual with an eating disorder cannot get help unless he or she realizes there is a problem. Recognizing and sharing with another that you suspect a problem sounds easier than it is. The next activity is designed to help students realize how hard it is to talk about eating disorders.

Distribute the **Privacy Circles** worksheet. Tell students to identify, in the center circle, the person in whom they feel most comfortable confiding. Explain that this is the person(s) in their life that they feel they can tell anything. Tell students to use initials or a secret code to indicate this person(s).

Then have students identify the second most confidential person or persons in the next circle from the center. Tell students to continue filling in the circles. Explain that as you move outward from the center, each of the circles represents someone in whom you would be less likely to confide.

Demonstrate on the **Privacy Circles** transparency by putting initials in each of the circles. Then explain to students each of the situations listed on the worksheet. Tell students to draw a line or lines from each situation to the circle that indicates the people with whom they would share that information or problem. Demonstrate on the transparency.

Ask students the following questions:

- Were there any situations that they felt they could share with (would not mind telling) anyone in their circles or people outside (not listed in) the circles?
- Were there situations that they would not share with anyone in the privacy circles?
- Which situations were more private to them?
- Why are some situations more private to some people than to others?

Tell students this exercise can help them identify people with whom they'd feel comfortable sharing information when they need help. Review each of the situations. Ask students where they could find help if they needed it for themselves, friends or family members.

Ask students if they can make any conclusions, based on this activity, about the difficulty of sharing information about eating disorders.

■ Show students the **Normal or Not?** transparency. Explain that the eating behaviors presented are in two categories. The first are normal behaviors for teenagers in response to weight concerns. The other behaviors indicate an eating disorder. Lead a class discussion of normal teenage dieting and weight control behaviors versus eating disorders. Ask students if there are other eating behaviors that could be added to the lists.

Explain that it's normal for teenagers to feel concerns about weight and to think of dieting. However, being obsessed with food, eating very small amounts (little-to-nothing) and bingeing on large amounts of food within a *planned* period of time followed by purging are *not* normal behaviors.

Emphasize that appropriate eating and exercise behaviors can help students control weight and develop a comfortable body image. Such behaviors can be maintained for a lifetime.

■ Tell students that eating disorders can be very difficult to treat. Emphasize the importance of prevention. Show students the **Prevention Pointers** transparency, and discuss each step. Emphasize that anyone thinking about weight loss should have a complete physical examination and professional advice before beginning a weight control program.

■ Distribute the **Problems Eating You?** worksheet. Tell students to think about a friend or family member they might be concerned about. Ask students to complete the questionnaire for this person.

Explain that this questionnaire can help students assess possible eating disorders or poor self-image. Tell students that if they answer yes to one or more questions, they might want to talk to a trusted adult about their concern.

Evaluation

Have students design a poster that illustrates at least one of the prevention behaviors for eating disorders. Encourage students to be creative and to emphasize the positive. Put posters up in the classroom or in the school hallways. Assess students' ability to present at least one of the key prevention points addressed in the lesson.

Assign a creative writing project. Have students write two case studies about two teenagers, one male and the other female. One of the case studies should describe a teen who potentially has an eating disorder and the other should describe normal teenage eating behaviors. Assess students' ability to differentiate between normal teenage eating behaviors and behaviors that indicate a possible eating disorder.

Follow-Up/ Extension

Have students prepare oral reports on a referral or treatment resource in your community for eating disorders.

Have students write to the organizations on **Help for Eating Disorders** to obtain the following information: name and address of resource; type of treatment used; whether treatment is inpatient or outpatient; cost of treatment. Have students report on their findings in a later class session.

Overcoming Eating Disorders

Teacher Background Information

The first step in overcoming an eating disorder is recognizing the problem—this step is also the hardest thing about this secretive disorder. The next step is obtaining help for the eating disorder.

Research by Dona M. Kagan (1987) indicates that compulsive eating among young women appears to be a response to environmental stress; but among young men, it may indicate deficiencies in a family system. Among more than 2,000 high school and college-age women studied, disordered eating habits were consistently associated with feelings of stress, failure and low self-esteem.

Males who tended to eat compulsively saw their families as relatively uncohesive and rigid. They were dissatisfied with their families and reported cold relationships with their parents.

The use and abuse of food as a response to stress is common among high school and college students. These years can be critical in forming lifetime habits. This may be the ideal time for teachers, counselors and parents to help young people cope with their feelings of stress and failure, their guilt concerning food abuse and their desire to be thin.

Adolescents need to identify other means of releasing stress besides overeating. They also need to understand that thinness and weight loss are not panaceas for feelings of inadequacy. Overeating does appear to be a very common stress response among otherwise normal young women.

Eating disorders can be successfully treated professionally with early detection and prompt competent treatment. Hospitalization may be avoided with outpatient therapeutic intervention treatment programs. Many victims learn to control the disordered behavior and thinking, rather than curing it.

Long-term residual effects of the disorders can cause problems. Approximately 10 percent of all victims of anorexia nervosa die from the illness or by committing suicide. People with eating disorders need to be reassured that they are loved for themselves and do not have to measure up to others to deserve love.

For more information on the types of treatments available for eating disorders, see the appendix.

Privacy Circles

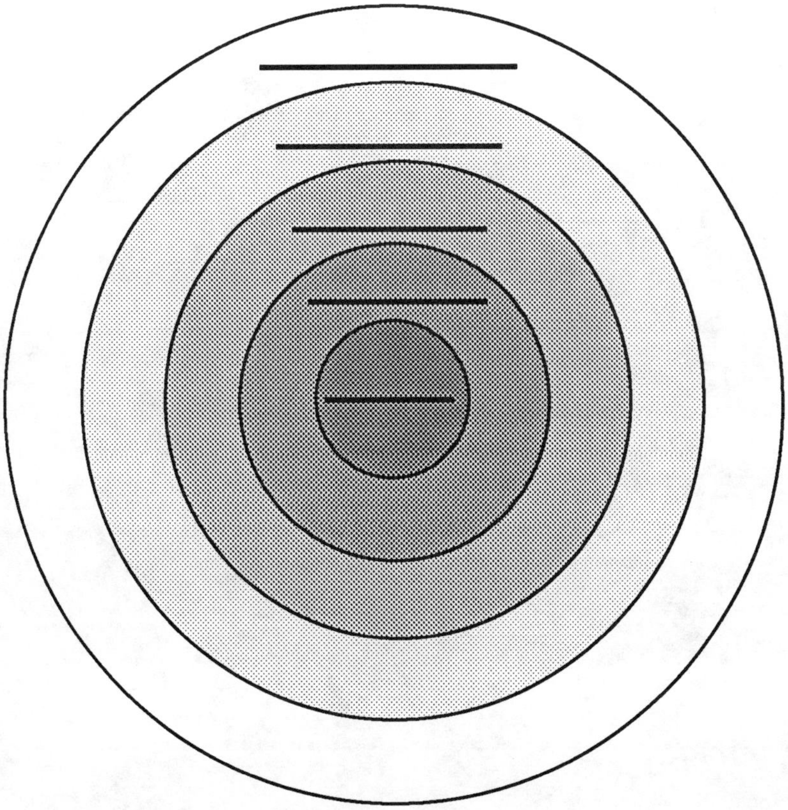

Situations

Who would you tell if...

- ○ you were in love
- ○ you got a new job
- ○ you cheated on a test
- ○ you had a friend who vomited in the school restroom to control his or her weight
- ○ your friend was stealing money from his or her parents or friends to buy food to gorge on
- ○ you had a friend who told you he or she was thinking about committing suicide
- ○ you had a friend who was starving him- or herself

Normal or Not?

Normal Eating Behavior	Eating Disorders
▷ eats reasonable portions of foods	➤ binges—eats large amounts of food within a short time
▷ usually eats a variety of foods at each meal	➤ plans eating binges
▷ eats the same types and amounts of food whether eating with others or alone	➤ when eating with others, eats nothing or plays with food
▷ eats enough to maintain a reasonable body weight	➤ uses purging or vomiting to get rid of food
▷ exercises regularly for fitness	➤ exercises to be slim and to use calories, may exercise too much
▷ *sometimes* eats as a response to stress	➤ is obsessed with thoughts of food
▷ *sometimes* diets in response to stress	➤ prefers to eat alone

Prevention Pointers

- ☞ Learn to like yourself, just as you are.
- ☞ Set realistic goals for yourself.
- ☞ Ask for support and encouragement from friends and family when life is stressful.
- ☞ Learn the basics of good nutrition and exercise.
- ☞ If you want to lose weight, talk to a doctor or a professional, registered dietitian who specializes in weight control.
- ☞ Seek adult help if you suspect a friend has an eating disorder problem.

STUDENT

Problems Eating You?

Directions: Read the following statements. Circle *Yes* if the statement describes someone you know, *No* if it doesn't apply.

I have a friend who...

1. constantly thinks about eating, weight and body size.......	**Yes**	**No**	**Not Sure**
2. feels anxious before eating..	**Yes**	**No**	**Not Sure**
3. is terrified of being overweight..	**Yes**	**No**	**Not Sure**
4. doesn't know when he or she is hungry............................	**Yes**	**No**	**Not Sure**
5. goes on eating binges and can't stop eating until he or she feels sick..	**Yes**	**No**	**Not Sure**
6. says he or she feels bloated or uncomfortable after eating.	**Yes**	**No**	**Not Sure**
7. spends a lot of time daydreaming about food...................	**Yes**	**No**	**Not Sure**
8. weighs her- or himself several times a day.......................	**Yes**	**No**	**Not Sure**
9. exercises too much and gets very uptight about his or her exercise plan.	**Yes**	**No**	**Not Sure**
10. says that being in control of food shows other people that he or she can control him- or herself.	**Yes**	**No**	**Not Sure**
11. has taken laxatives or forced her- or himself to vomit after eating.	**Yes**	**No**	**Not Sure**
12. is letting food control his or her life.	**Yes**	**No**	**Not Sure**
13. says he or she feels very guilty after eating.	**Yes**	**No**	**Not Sure**
14. eats when feeling nervous, anxious, lonely or depressed.	**Yes**	**No**	**Not Sure**
15. doesn't think he or she looks good in his or her clothes...	**Yes**	**No**	**Not Sure**
16. seems uptight about his or her weight and appearance when around other people.	**Yes**	**No**	**Not Sure**
17. seems resentful when a friend or family member suggests he or she use a little willpower.	**Yes**	**No**	**Not Sure**
18. tries to diet for a definite period of time, but never seems to make it all the way.	**Yes**	**No**	**Not Sure**
19. avoids parties and get-togethers because she or he feels self-conscious about weight.	**Yes**	**No**	**Not Sure**
20. has a problem with overeating and doesn't know what to do.	**Yes**	**No**	**Not Sure**

HELP FOR EATING DISORDERS

National Association of Anorexia Nervosa and Associated Disorders
(ANAD)
P.O. Box 7
Highland Park, Illinois 60035
(312) 831-3438

Anorexia Nervosa and Related Eating Disorders, Inc.
P.O. Box 5102
Eugene, Oregon 97405
(503) 344-1144

American Anorexia/ Bulimia Association, Inc.
133 Cedar Lane
Teaneck, New Jersey 07666
(201) 836-1800

National Anorexic Aid Society, Inc.
P.O. Box 29461
5796 Karl Road
Columbus, Ohio 43229
(614) 895-2009
(614) 436-1112

Center for the Study of Anorexia and Bulimia
1 West 91st Street
New York, New York 10024
(212) 595-3449

Bulimia, Anorexia Self-Help
6125 Clayton Avenue
Suite 215
St. Louis, Missouri 63139

Contact the local medical society, mental health center or mental health association. Or, there may be a local chapter of these organizations in your area.

LESSON 5

WEIGHT CONTROL PROBLEMS

Objectives

Students will be able to differentiate between effective and ineffective weight control programs.

Students will be able to identify community resources for weight control.

Time

Two class periods.

Overview

Numerous weight loss programs promise quick and easy weight loss to American dieters. However, research indicates that as many as 95 percent of the people who use a weight loss program will fail, because they are unable either to lose the weight or to maintain the weight loss.

In this lesson, students consider and discuss a variety of weight loss programs. They work in small groups to research some programs available locally and prepare class reports.

Teacher Materials and Preparation

HAVE:

✓ Overhead projector.

COPY:

✓ **Weigh It** worksheet, one for each group of four or five students.
✓ **Weighing the Balance** worksheet, one for each student.

MAKE:

✓ Transparency of **Want to Lose Weight? No Problem!**

REVIEW:

✓ **Weight Control Programs** ***Teacher Background Information.***

Procedure

■ Ask students: Do you know someone who claims to have tried every diet known, but still can't lose excess weight?

Explain that fad diets backfire, and people get caught in the dieting cycle. For example, someone may go on a quick-weight-loss diet and lose seven pounds in two days. However, what this person has really lost is a pound or two of fat and five or six pounds of water, muscle and minerals. When she or he goes off the diet, his or her body will regain the needed water and minerals.

Note that weight lost as muscle is frequently regained as fat. Over time, the body is composed of less muscle and more fat, even if weight remains the same. Fat tissue requires less energy to maintain itself than does muscle tissue, so the body uses even fewer calories.

The basal metabolic rate (how fast the body uses calories while resting) declines. Then the dieter has to eat even less in order to lose weight, so the next diet cycle is even harder.

The weight loss and gain that results from fad diets is called the yo-yo syndrome. It is very stressful for the body to adjust to such rapid changes.

Tell students that this dieting cycle is also psychologically stressful. It often leads to alternate bingeing and fasting behavior. When a dieter goes off a quick-weight-loss diet and regains weight, the dieter feels that he or she has failed again and becomes depressed.

To ward off these feelings of depression, the dieter may overeat or binge. This behavior is followed by feelings of guilt or remorse for having lost control. Once again, the dieter fasts to regain control or to punish him- or herself and the cycle of fasting and bingeing continues.

Suggest to students that weight is an invalid measure of success. The percent of total body fat is more important for health *and* appearance. Healthy adults should have approximately 16 percent body fat for males and 25 percent body fat for females. Body fat can be measured in a hydrostatic (underwater) test or by the use of skinfold calipers. The ratio of fat to muscle and your waist to hip ratio will determine your healthy weight. (A physical education specialist, physician or registered dietician should be able to perform this measure reliably.)

■ Show students the **Want to Lose Weight? No Problem!** transparency. Conduct a short discussion of the common advertising claim that losing weight is easy, as the models in this transparency are claiming.

Use the **Weight Control Programs *Teacher Background Information*** as a guide to a discussion of effective versus ineffective weight control programs and methods. Ask students which categories some diets they are familiar with fit into.

■ Divide class into small groups. Distribute the **Weigh It** worksheet. Tell groups to research three types of weight control programs. Have students contact local programs in the community to investigate responses to the questions on the worksheet. (Check the Yellow Pages of the phone book.)

Note: Some programs may be very secretive about their products and programs. Tell students that learning to question the worth of such programs is an important consumer health experience.

Tell groups to report what they learn about these programs to the class. When groups have made their reports, lead a class discussion comparing the various programs.

Students will probably find that all of the programs have one thing in common—claims of long-term success. Note that most diets see good weight loss at the beginning. Then most people begin to feel less motivated after several weeks; they get bored with the food or frustrated with not eating.

Ask students if they know individuals who have tried these weight loss programs. Ask about their success and long-term weight loss.

Most dietitians, medical and nutrition experts claim that at least 90 percent of dieters are likely to eventually gain back all or part of or more than the weight they lost. Stress that people who need to lose weight need to change their eating and exercise patterns for the rest of their lives.

Many diet professionals say that a program such as Weight Watchers is less regimented and probably more effective than many other diet plans. Although weight loss on such a plan is more gradual than the quick loss that accompanies liquid diets, the slower loss rate helps people establish better eating habits.

Emphasize that a plan that does not include exercise is likely to fail. All the enrollment-style diets provide exercise recommendations, although they usually don't include exercise classes.

Lead students to conclude that the perfect diet is probably not a diet at all. Eating less, eating right and exercising more are the keys to long-term health and high energy.

Evaluation

Distribute the **Weighing the Balance** worksheet, and have students complete it. Assess students' ability to differentiate key items that typify the components of effective vs. ineffective weight loss programs.

Evaluate group reports and students' responses in class discussion to assess student ability to identify weight control programs in the community.

Weight Control Programs

Teacher Background Information

There are four categories of weight control programs:

1. **Limited calories with a balanced food intake.**
   These diets meet nutritional and caloric needs, and the energy balance is reasonable. Weight Watchers is one such program that does not require use of special formulas, pills or other products. Richard Simmons also offers a diet of moderation and balance, which is nutritionally adequate.

2. **Reduced calories with diet changes and special foods**
   High-fiber diets are an example of these weight control programs. The F-Plan diet is based on the assumption that fiber-rich foods are filling but contain fewer calories and promote rapid passage of food through the intestines. Proponents of this diet assert that fewer calories are absorbed by the body. The Pritikin Program emphasizes an extremely low-fat diet that is low in calories and high in fiber.

3. ***Magic* pills**
   These programs emphasize vitamin supplements or diet pills such as appetite suppressants (for example, the over-the-counter drug, phenylpropanolamine). Or they may claim that a magic food such as grapefruit will lead to speedy weight loss.

   Be wary of novelty diets that emphasize consumption of a particular nutrient, food or combinations of foods that will oxidize body fat, inhibit voluntary food intake, remove toxic products from the body, increase metabolic rate and result in quick and major weight loss.

   Such diets include the grapefruit diet, pineapple diet, strawberries-and-cream diet, pumpkin-carrot diet, egg and orange diet and ice cream diet, which all advocate reduced calorie intake. Initial weight loss is due to immediate water loss. These diets give little attention to the need to include adequate amounts of all known essential nutrients and to develop a long-range nutritional and activity program designed to maintain desirable body weight.

4. **Unbalanced intake of carbohydrate, protein or fat**
   Diets low in carbohydrate and fat cause chemical changes in the body. The major appeal is the diuretic (fluid loss through urination) effect during the first ten to fourteen days. This effect provides a transient weight loss that can be dramatic, but that weight loss can be quickly regained.

   The protein-sparing fast restricts calories to 300-400 Kcals/day or a high-protein supplement. When the body's glucose stores are depleted during a fast, the body begins to make ketones from fat rather than provide glucose from the protein's amino acids. Lean body mass is apparently conserved while weight reduction is achieved.

   These fasts may be hazardous. People on liquid protein diets have suffered heart arrhythmias and died. Close medical supervision is *always* advised with these types of programs. They are not appropriate for people who need to lose only a few pounds.

The Beverly Hills diet is based on claims that raw fruits, vegetables, seeds and plant juices are sources of enzymes that help melt accumulated fat cells. This unsound diet promotes binge eating. It is so restrictive that it could not be followed for any length of time.

Some low-protein, low-fat regimens are based on low-calorie food combinations (e.g., bananas and skim milk). They claim they require more calories to digest than they provide in energy to the body. (Incidentally, about 10 percent of the calories from food are required by the body to digest that food.) If weight loss does occur, it results from reduced calorie intake due to boredom.

Misconceptions about balanced nutrition can also turn a well-balanced vegetarian diet into a nutrient-deficient program. The Zen Macrobiotic Diet claims that there are unhealthy Yang foods (meat, eggs, fish) and unwholesome Yin foods (sugar, dairy products, fruits and vegetables). These foods are gradually limited and eliminated until the diet consists solely of brown rice and tea. This diet will induce weight loss, followed by malnutrition and eventual death.

Enrollment diets fall into the four categories of weight control programs. They are estimated to be a multibillion-dollar industry. Each one offers a special hook to attract the 100 million overweight Americans. There are three basic types of enrollment-style diets:

1. **Liquid or supplemented fast diets**. Typically, these are medically supervised by the dieter's personal physician or one designated by the diet facility. The regimen involves an initial period of abstaining from solid food and subsisting on the low-calorie, high-nutrient liquid supplement. A normal, balanced diet is then gradually reintroduced during a period of counseling and behavior modification. Optifast and the Cambridge Plan are typical examples of these diets.

2. **Prepackaged food diets**. The Nutri/System and Jenny Craig plans belong to this category. They provide dieters with full menus of prepackaged, low-calorie foods that dieters prepare themselves. They offer periodic group meetings and behavior modification classes with diet counselors.

3. **Low-calorie, real food diets**. The Diet Center and Weight Watchers are examples of this category. Participants attend meetings, behavior modification classes and group support sessions while adhering to a varied low-calorie diet of foods available at a grocery store.

Want to Lose Weight? No Problem!

Which programs are likely to work?

STUDENT

Weigh It

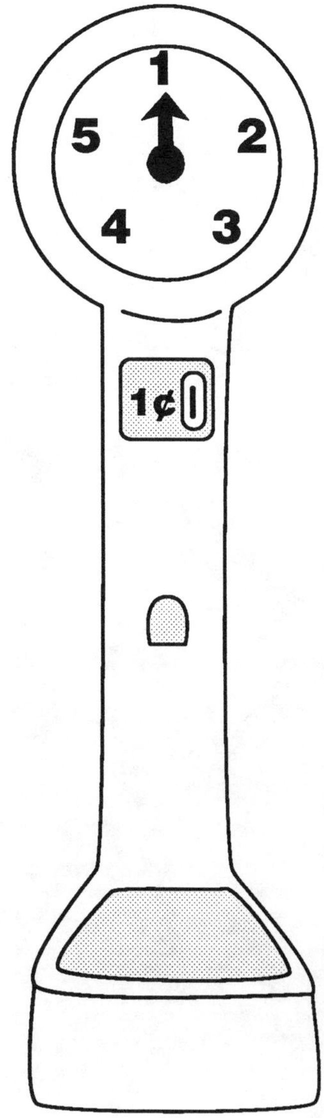

Directions: With your group, select a weight loss diet program or diet plan to investigate. Answer the following questions. Then rate the plan on the scale that follows.

1. What is the name of diet program or diet plan?

   ____

2. If you visited a diet program site, what is the address?

   ____

3. Who did you speak to about the program?

   ____

4. What is the phone number of the program?

   ( ) ______________________________

5. What is the cost of the program or diet plan?

   ____

6. Are discounts available for students? (circle) Yes No

7. Is there an additional cost for special food, special formulas or diet supplements? (circle) Yes No

8. Is health insurance accepted as payment in full or as partial payment? (circle) Yes No

9. Are there any restrictions to program or diet plan? (circle) Yes No
   If yes, what are they? ______________________________

10. Briefly describe the diet program or plan.

    ____

    ____

    ____

Use the following rating scale to rate the program your group reviewed.

5 = Superior
4 = Above average
3 = Average
2 = Below average
1 = Inadequate

Criteria	*Rating*
The diet program or plan is healthy.	5 4 3 2 1
The program is easy to use.	5 4 3 2 1
The cost of the program is reasonable for the average person.	5 4 3 2 1
The program could be used for a lifetime.	5 4 3 2 1
The program promotes steady, reasonable weight loss.	5 4 3 2 1
The program offers a maintenance plan to help keep the weight off.	5 4 3 2 1
The program suggests a variety of fresh, natural foods.	5 4 3 2 1
The program promotes long-term changes in eating habits.	5 4 3 2 1
The program encourages regular exercise.	5 4 3 2 1

Scoring: Add your scores for each of these criteria and divide by 9 to determine an *overall rating* of the healthfulness of this diet program or plan. Circle the rating number on the scale on the previous page.

Weighing the Balance

Directions: List two or three factors of a good weight loss program on the *What Works* side of the scale. On the *What Won't Work* side, list two or three factors of ineffective weight loss programs.

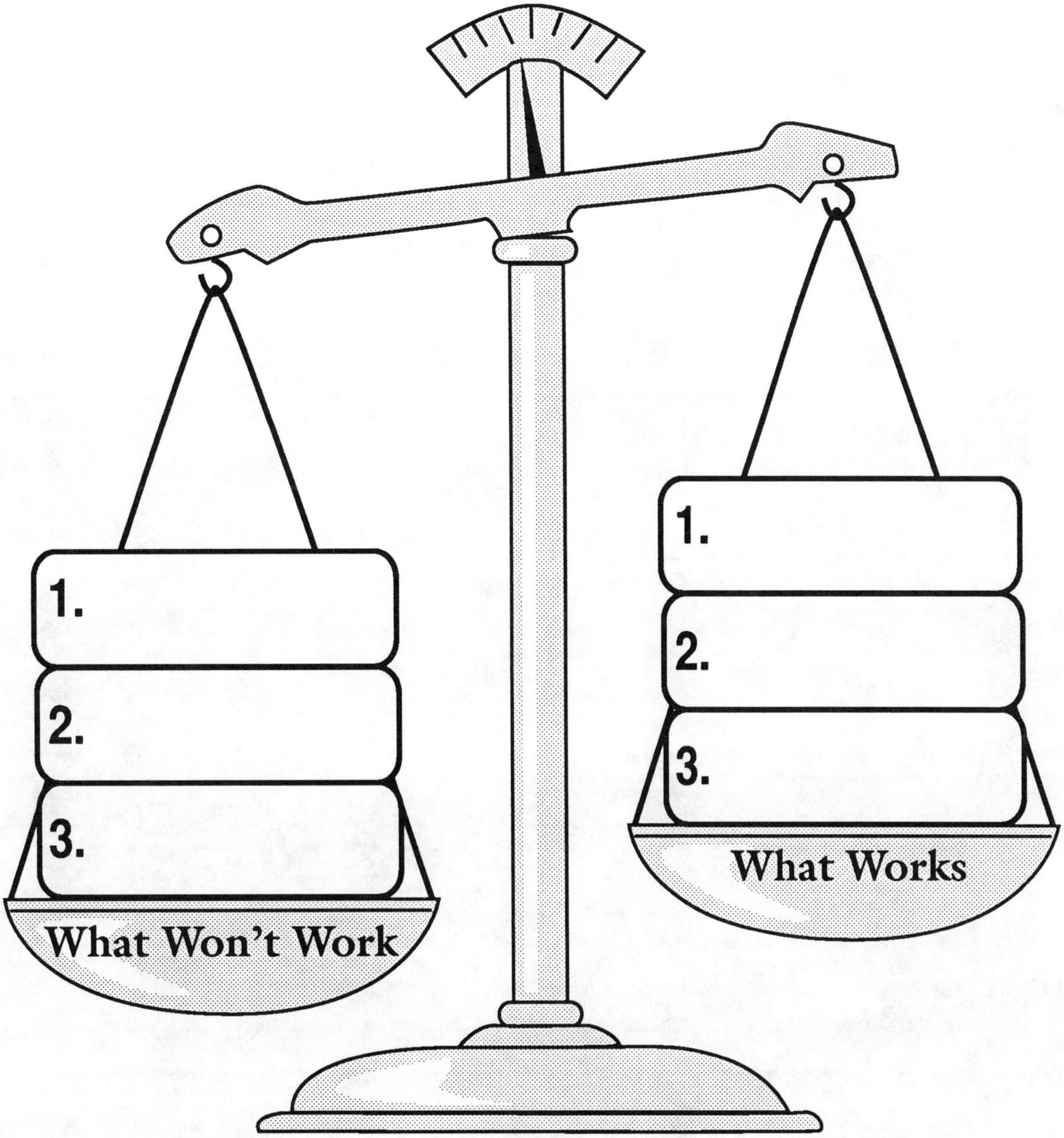

LESSON 6

SENSIBLE EATING HABITS

Objectives

Students will be able to identify sensible eating and exercise behaviors.

Students will be able to identify society's influences on eating behaviors.

Time

One class period.

Overview

Regular exercise and healthy eating habits can enhance students' health and lifestyle. Changes students make now will improve their health for a lifetime.

In this lesson, students study some suggestions for making healthy changes in eating and exercise behaviors. The lesson concludes with a look at some of our society's conflicting messages about eating and body image.

Note: This lesson cannot substitute for a comprehensive nutrition or fitness program. Fitness is dealt with in another module in the Contemporary Health Series, *Entering Adulthood: Moving into Fitness*. For a comprehensive nutrition module, see *Into Adolescence: A Menu for Good Health,* also part of the Comprehensive Health Series. The latter module is intended for middle school students, but would be appropriate for high school students who have not had a nutrition program in lower grades.

Teacher Materials and Preparation

HAVE:

✓ Overhead projector.
✓ Blank transparencies *or* butcher paper, two pieces.
✓ Transparency marker *or* colored markers.

COPY:

✓ **Here's to Your Health** student information sheet, one for each student.
✓ **Your Eating Habits** worksheet, one for each student.
✓ **Exercise—It's Your Choice** worksheet, one for each student.

MAKE:

✓ Transparency of **Guidelines for Healthy Eating**.

Procedure

■ Tell students that good nutrition is important for health. Point out that no single meal or type of food supplies all of the nutrients the body needs. Suggest that eating a variety of healthy foods and enjoying a variety of activities are the best ways to develop and maintain a healthy body.

Distribute the **Here's to Your Health** student information sheet. Show students the **Guidelines for Healthy Eating** transparency. Tell students that these seven dietary guidelines were developed to help people make wise food choices. Have students read the additional information from the worksheet as you review the guidelines.

■ Distribute the **Your Eating Habits** worksheet, and have students complete it.

Tell students to compare their eating habits to the suggestions on the **Guidelines for Healthy Eating** transparency. (Leave transparency showing for this discussion.) Ask if they see any areas that they'd like to change.

Ask students to think about ways to change eating habits. Discuss some of the following changes:

- If you often nibble while doing other things, try to plan your meals and snacks ahead of time.
- Decide to eat only at the kitchen table or dining room table when at home.
- If candy bars from the vending machine at school are a problem, bring low-calorie snacks from home.
- Switch from sodas containing sugar to milk (low-fat or skim), fruit juice or water.
- If you often eat because you're bored, frustrated or stressed, think of other activities to get your mind off food—jog, call a friend or walk the dog.
- If rich desserts are a problem, try fresh fruit instead.
- If topping on your baked potato is a source of extra calories, try less topping or plain yogurt instead of sour cream.
- If you're used to the flavor of whole milk but want less fat and fewer calories, try low-fat milk or skim milk (combine half whole milk and half skim milk first, to adjust for taste).

Discuss the concept of *nutrient density*—some foods contain an abundance of nutrients in proportion to calories. The opposite of nutrient-dense foods are *empty-calorie* foods—foods that are high in calories but lack nutrients like protein, complex carbohydrates, vitamins and minerals.

Nutrient-dense foods include milk, cheese, yogurt, lean meats, fish, poultry, nuts, seeds, eggs, dark green and yellow vegetables, fruits, beans, rice and whole grain or enriched breads and cereals. Ask students for examples of empty calorie foods. These will include sodas, candy bars, chips and other similar foods.

■ Tell students that physical activity, combined with good nutrition, improves overall fitness. It has other pluses, too. For example, exercise can help relieve tensions that often lead to overeating. Point out that students don't have to be athletes to make physical activity count.

Distribute the **Exercise—It's Your Choice** worksheet. Tell students that it's best to make slow, steady changes in activity level. Point out that there are lots of little ways to improve fitness. Walk or bicycle instead of drive, use the stairs instead of the elevator, stand rather than sit.

Tell students to look at the suggestions on the worksheet for ways to increase levels of physical activity. Ask students to check the activities that are best for them. Suggest that students think of other activities that interest them.

■ Acknowledge that it can be difficult to change eating behaviors. Tell students that our society sends some conflicting messages about body image and eating behaviors. Divide the class into two groups. Tell students in one group to discuss our society's pressures and influences to eat. Tell the other group to discuss the pressures *not* to eat. Point out that there are social, cultural, emotional and economic pressures.

Tell groups to list the pressures and influences on a piece of butcher paper or a transparency. Ask them to give examples of each of the pressures and influences they list. Then have each group report their responses to the class.

Many of the pressures not to eat were discussed in the earlier lessons on body image. Some examples of the pressures to eat include:

- going out to eat with friends
- eating birthday cake at a party
- snacking while studying for an exam
- television advertisements for donuts, candy, cakes, fast foods, etc.

Lead a class discussion of the conflicts that arise from these different messages. For example: Television shows that star people with lean well-proportioned bodies may have commercials for empty-calorie foods. Magazines may feature new recipes for high-calorie desserts and new diet regimes in the same issues.

Ask students how they cope with these conflicting messages. Suggest that making gradual changes in both eating behaviors and exercise levels is the best approach to improving health and energy. Tell students that changes they make now will offer them benefits for a lifetime.

Evaluation

Tell students to look at their responses on the **Your Eating Habits** and **Exercise—It's Your Choice** worksheets. Have students write a paragraph describing two changes they could make in their eating and exercise behaviors that would improve their health.

In the paragraph, students should also list several of society's influences on their body image and eating behaviors. Assess students' ability to identify conflicting pressures related to eating and body image.

for your information

Here's to Your Health

1. **Eat a variety of foods.** You need about 40 different nutrients to stay healthy. The best way to be sure you get all of them is to eat a variety of foods, including breads, cereals and grains, fruits and vegetables, meat, poultry, fish, eggs, dry beans and peas, and dairy products such as milk, cheese and yogurt. Drink plenty of water, too—six to eight glasses a day.

2. **Maintain healthy weight.** Healthy weight is different for each person. Improving your eating and exercise habits can help you maintain a weight that is healthy for you. Your overall ratio of fat to muscle and your waist to hips ratio determine your healthy weight. The focus is on fitness and exercise, not on fatness.

3. **Choose a diet low in fat, saturated fat and cholesterol.**
   - Choose lean meats and trim the fat.
   - Remove skin from poultry and fish.
   - Use skim or low-fat dairy products.
   - Broil, bake or boil instead of frying.
   - Use less butter and cream.
   - Reduce your intake of lard, palm and coconut oils (found in many prepared foods).
   - Eat fewer breaded and deep-fried foods, egg yolks and organ meats (such as liver).

4. **Choose a diet with plenty of vegetables, fruits and grain products.**
   - Whole grain breads and cereals, vegetables and fruits are good sources of fiber and other nutrients and should be included in the diet more frequently.

5. **Use sugars only in moderation.**
   - Eat fewer candies, cakes, cookies, muffins, etc.
   - Try fresh or frozen fruit for dessert.
   - Read labels for sugar content. Sucrose, glucose, fructose, honey, dextrose, corn syrups and other syrups are all kinds of sugar.
   - Drink water or fruit juice instead of sugar-sweetened sodas.

6. **Use salt and sodium only in moderation.**
   - Don't add salt in cooking or at the table.
   - Try seasoning foods with herbs, lemon juice, garlic, onion powder, etc.
   - Limit salty snacks like chips, pretzels, etc.
   - Check labels for sodium amounts—500 milligrams (500 mg.) is the recommended daily allowance for adolescents and adults.

7. **(For adults only.) If you drink alcohol, do so in moderation.**

U.S. Departments of Agriculture and Health and Human Services. *Dietary Guidelines for Americans,* 3rd ed. 1990.

Guidelines for Healthy Eating

1. Eat a variety of foods.
2. Maintain healthy weight.
3. Choose a diet low in fat, saturated fat and cholesterol.
4. Choose a diet with plenty of vegetables, fruits and grain products.
5. Use sugars only in moderation.
6. Use salt and sodium only in moderation.
7. (For adults only.) If you drink alcoholic beverages, do so in moderation.

Your Eating Habits

Directions: Think about your eating patterns and habits. What, how much, when, where and why do you eat? For each of the following questions, check the answer that best describes your eating patterns.

What do I usually eat?

- ☐ A varied and balanced diet that includes only moderate amounts of fat, sugar and salt
- ☐ Deep-fat fried and breaded foods
- ☐ Extras, such as salad dressings, potato toppings, spreads, sauces and gravies
- ☐ Sweets and rich desserts such as candies, cakes, pies
- ☐ Snack foods high in fat and sodium, such as chips

How much do I usually eat?

- ☐ A single small serving
- ☐ A large serving
- ☐ Two servings or more

When do I usually eat?

- ☐ At mealtimes only
- ☐ While preparing meals or clearing the table
- ☐ After school
- ☐ While watching television or participating in other activities
- ☐ At school breaks
- ☐ Anytime

Where do I usually eat?

- ☐ At the kitchen table or dining room table
- ☐ At restaurants or fast-food places
- ☐ In front of the television or while reading
- ☐ Where I am preparing the food
- ☐ Wherever I happen to be when I'm hungry

Why do I usually eat?

- ☐ It's time to eat.
- ☐ I'm starved.
- ☐ Foods look tempting.
- ☐ Everyone else is eating.
- ☐ Food will get thrown away if I don't eat it.

(Adapted from U.S. Department of Agriculture, Human Nutrition Information Service. 1986. Nutrition and your health: Dietary guidelines for Americans. *Home and garden bulletin* No. 232-2.)

Exercise—It's Your Choice

Directions: Check or circle the activities that are best suited to your interests. Then make a plan for yourself.

☆ Use the stairs instead of the elevator.

☆ Put more energy into everyday activities (e.g., walk instead of using a car or bus).

☆ Take several one-minute stretch breaks during the day.

☆ Take a walk each day at lunchtime or after school.

☆ Attend an aerobics or other exercise class.

☆ Develop a do-it-yourself home exercise program alone or with friends.

☆ Set up a regular weekly schedule for activities such as running, swimming, tennis, roller-skating, etc.

☆ Set up a daily routine of walking, bicycling or jogging.

☆ Play basketball at the gym or school or at home.

☆ Join a sports team or league.

☆ Go dancing.

APPENDIX

A

TREATMENT OF EATING DISORDERS

There are a variety of treatments available for eating disorders. Depending on the severity of the disorder, hospitalization may be required. Dehydration, electrolyte imbalance, distorted thinking, heart arrhythmias and other problems associated with starvation require immediate hospitalization. Some programs are outpatient only and may offer one or more of the following treatment methods.

Some areas offer special programs for treating eating disorders. Some programs are inpatient in regular hospitals; others are located in psychiatric hospitals. Some hospital programs stress weight gain, others stress therapy.

In addition to medical intervention to help patients regain lost weight, programs must include a combination of therapeutic interventions. These interventions should focus on the individual and family. Long-term counseling is important.

Treatment of psychosocial eating disorders is needed for a continuous time, months or even years. Several treatments alone and in combination have been successful in the treatment of eating disorders. They include the following therapies:

- *Cognitive-behavioral therapy*—Food diaries and self-reported eating habits and behaviors help identify and monitor both positive and negative behaviors. Behavior modification techniques are used to reward normal eating behavior and discourage self-starvation and bingeing and purging.

- *Individual therapy*—In combination with other treatments, psychological treatment can help the individual correct perceptions of body image; decrease feelings of depression, guilt and anxiety; enhance esteem and assertiveness and stress management skills; and monitor weight. Pharmaceutical (drug) treatment may also be used.

- *Group psychotherapy* may help reduce a sense of isolation and secrecy. This treatment may be especially effective for bulimics. Guided by professionals, this can be a useful and powerful adjunct to recovery.

- *Family therapy*—The dynamics of the family play a pivotal role in the development of eating disorders. Therefore, family members, including parents, siblings, spouses and significant others, must be involved in the treatment plan. They should be encouraged to provide a supportive recovery environment for the patient.

- *Drug therapy*—Since depression and anxiety accompany the eating disorders, some medications may be prescribed as part of the treatment program. Vitamin and mineral supplements may also be prescribed. Although the majority of research on eating disorders has emphasized drug therapy, medications have given false hope to patients with eating disorders.

- *Bibliotherapy*—Reading real-life accounts of other people with eating disorders may be a prescribed part of a treatment program.

- *Reality imaging*—Photographs and videotapes and computer imaging are often used to help the patient correct a distorted body image, especially when the body form is emaciated but perceived as fat.

- *Guided imagery* teaches patients to shift their focus from perceived body flaws to positive attributes.

- *Biofeedback training and relaxation techniques* may help a person overcome stress and gain control of his or her feelings.

- *Education*—Nutritionists, registered dietitians and other diet specialists work with therapists and physicians to teach the patient appropriate healthy eating habits and educate him or her about nutrition.

- *Hypnotherapy*—Limited success has been experienced using hypnosis as a treatment for eating disorders, because hypnosis requires the patient to relinquish control, which is something most eating disorder patients resist.

- *Self-help or support groups* are an adjunct to primary treatment. Through sharing experiences, members give mutual emotional support, exchange information and diminish feelings of isolation. Services may include information on symptoms and treatment, lists of therapists, newsletters, book reviews and bibliographies.

APPENDIX B

GLOSSARY

Addiction—Physical or psychological condition of dependence on a drug.

Amenorrhea—Absence or cessation of menstruation.

Anorexia—Loss of appetite. A term incorrectly used to describe individuals with Anorexia Nervosa, since loss of appetite is rare among these individuals.

Anorexia Nervosa—Self starvation associated with emotional, maladaptive behavior; an eating disorder characterized by a psychological condition with progressive weight loss, fear of weight gain, a cycle of repeated ritualistic rigid behavior focused on food, and a distorted body image that can lead to death.

Body image—Recognition of what the individual is, physically and biologically, is a prerequisite for the successful achievement of a mature personal identity. The development of a body image and identity acceptable to the adolescent may be impaired, however, by normal, unavoidable variations from the prevailing cultural stereotype of masculinity and femininity. Body image also may fail to evolve appropriately because of conflicts about one's sexual anatomy and functions, which may be unresolved. (Committee on Adolescence, 1968).

Bulimia—An eating disorder characterized by recurrent episodes of binge eating and secretive purging, using self-induced vomiting, abuse of laxatives and diuretics, fasting and overexercising. This term is used commonly in lay, medical and health publications. However, the *DSM-III-R (Diagnostic & Statistical Manual of Mental Disorders,* 3rd ed., 1987) uses the term *Bulimia Nervosa* to describe this disorder; and *Bulimarexia* is also used to describe this binge-purge cycle (Boskind-White, M. and W.C. White. 1987. *Bulimarexia: The binge/purge cycle.* 2nd ed. London: W.W. Norton & Co. Ltd.).

Cathartic—Often used interchangeably with *laxative;* stronger, faster-acting or higher-dose laxatives.

Diuretics—Drugs that help relieve the body of excess water; sodium, potassium and other electrolytes may also be lost and need to be replaced.

Drug—Substance or medicine that changes or alters the function of the body or mind.

Dysmorphophobia—An obsession in which people fixate on a body flaw and blow it out of proportion.

Empty calorie food—Foods high in calories but lacking in nutrient value (e.g., soft drinks, cookies, cakes, candy and many snack foods).

Laxative—Substance that produces evacuation of the bowel; includes cathartics, purgatives and laxatives.

Laxative abuse—Use of laxatives for the purpose of weight control.

Mental-emotional traits—Characteristics that relate to feelings, perceptions, experiences, personal relationships, inner conflicts, sexuality, impulses, moodiness and coping mechanisms.

Mental health—The capacity to cope with life situations, grow emotionally through them, develop to the fullest potential and grow in awareness and consciousness. Mental health is feeling good about oneself, accepting physical appearance, being content with life and gaining inner peace. It is also the active seeking of experiences that promote peak mental states (Laing and Breuss, 1989).

Nutrient density—Refers to foods that contain an abundance of nutrients in proportion to the amount of calories that are provided.

Personal characteristics—Those traits or characteristics that make up the individual being, including physical, mental-emotional, social and personality traits. Personal characteristics change during adolescence and early adulthood.

Personality traits—Attitudes, habits, emotions and thoughts that produce a characteristic way of behaving.

Physical traits—Characteristics that relate to personal appearance. During adolescence, changes in physical characteristics include growth spurts, development of sex glands and appearance of secondary sex characteristics, accompanied by the desire to look normal, acceptable and pleasing to self and others.

Purgative—Often used interchangeably with *laxative;* stronger, faster-acting or higher-dose laxatives.

Purging—Self-induced vomiting and laxative abuse.

Self-concept—Refers to what the individual thinks, feels and believes about him- or herself. It is her or his understanding of personal abilities, values and feelings.

Self-esteem—The judgment a person makes and usually maintains with regard to him- or herself. It expresses an attitude of approval or disapproval and indicates the extent to which a person believes him- or herself capable, significant, successful and worthy (Laing and Breuss, 1989). Feelings of self-worth; judgments about ourselves, positive and negative.

Or put another way, the California Task Force to Promote Self-Esteem and Personal and Social Responsibility defined self-esteem as "appreciating my own worth and importance and having the character to be accountable for myself and to act responsibly toward others."

Social traits—Characteristics that provide a sense of self and others. Goal setting, peer group affiliation, building relationships and practicing interpersonal skills are social characteristics.

APPENDIX C

REFERENCES

American College Health Association. 1990. *Eating disorders.* Rockville, MD.

American Psychiatric Association. 1987. *Diagnostic and statistical manual of mental disorders (DSM-III-R)*, pp. 65-69. 3rd ed., rev. Washington, DC.

Anorexia nervosa and bulimia. 1986. Eugene, OR: Anorexia Nervosa and Related Eating Disorders.

Bayer, A. E. and D. H. Baker. 1985. Eating disorders: Anorexia and bulimia. Santa Cruz, CA: Network Publications.

Boskind-White, M. and W. C. White. 1990. Paper presented at the national convention of the American College Health Association, San Antonio.

Bryant, C. A., A. Courtney, B. A. Markesbery and K. M. DeWalt. *The cultural feast: An introduction to food and society.* 1985. St. Paul, MN: West Publishing.

California Task Force to Promote Self-Esteem and Personal and Social Responsibility. 1990. *Toward a state of esteem*. Sacramento, CA: California State Department of Education.

Committee on Adolescence, Group for the Advancement of Psychiatry. 1968. *Normal adolescence*. New York: Charles Scribner's Sons.

Crooks, R. and K. Baur. 1990. *Our sexuality,* pp. 629-631. 4th ed. Redwood City, CA: Benjamin/Cummings.

Desmond, S. M., J. H. Price, C. Hallinan and D. Smith. 1989. Black and White adolescents' perceptions of their weight. *Journal of School Health* 59, no. 8 (October): 353-358.

Eating disorders program self-assessment. 1983. Glendale, CA: Glendale Adventist Medical Center—Chevy Chase.

Greenberg, J. S. and D. Pargman. 1986. *Physical fitness: A wellness approach,* pp. 206-207. Englewood Cliffs, NJ: Prentice-Hall.

Guillum, R. F. 1987. Overweight and obesity in Black women: A review of published data from the National Center for Health Statistics. *Journal of the National Medical Association* 70:865-871.

Huenemann, R. L., M. C. Hampton, A. R. Behuke et al. 1974. *Teenage nutrition and physique*. Springfield, IL: Charles C. Thomas.

Kagan, D. M. 1987. Is adolescent compulsive eating and dieting overdiagnosed? *Educational Horizons* (Spring): 130-132.

Laing, S. J. and C. E. Bruess. 1989. *Entering adulthood: Connecting health, communication and self-esteem*. Santa Cruz, CA: Network Publications.

Lerner, R. M. and D. F. Hultsch. 1983. *Human development: A life-span perspective*. New York: McGraw-Hill.

McKee, G., ed. 1987. *Nutrition and the M.D. Special Report: Obesity and other eating disorders*. Van Nuys, CA: PM, Inc.

Mitchell, J. E., L. I. Bontacoff, D. Hatsukami, R. L. Pyle and E. D. Eckert. 1986. Laxative abuse as a variant of bulimia. *Journal of Nervous and Mental Disorders* 174, no. 3: 174-176.

Mott, P. 1989. Nutrition: The diet dilemma. *The Los Angeles Times Magazine: The Good Health Magazine* (October 8): 62-71.

National Health Interview Survey. 1986. National Center for Health Statistics.

Patterson, C. M., D. P. Whelan, C. L. Rock and T. J. Lyon. 1989. *Nutrition and eating disorders: Guidelines for the patient with anorexia nervosa and bulimia nervosa.* Van Nuys, CA: PM, Inc.

Schneller, J. 1990. Nobody's perfect: Why college women often look to the mirror to find themselves. *In View* (May/June): 10-13.

U. S. Department of Health and Human Services, Public Health Service. 1990. *Healthy People 2000: National Health Promotion and Disease Prevention Objectives.* Washington, DC.

Vanin, J. R. and K. E. Saylor. 1989. Laxative abuse: A hazardous habit for weight control. *Journal of College Health* 37 (March): 227-230.

What you need to know about eating disorders: Anorexia nervosa and bulimia nervosa. 1989. National Anorexic Society.

What you should know about self-esteem. 1990. South Deerfield, MA: Channing L. Bete.

Wise, J. K. and S. K. Wise. 1985. *The overeaters: Eating styles and personality.* New York: Human Sciences Press.